Zingerman's Guide to Better Bacon

This Book Belongs to:

Zingerman's

Guide to Better

STORIES OF
PORK BELLIES,
HUSH PUPPIES,
ROCK 'N' ROLL MUSIC
AND BACON FAT
MAYONNAISE

Bacon

ARI WEINZWEIG

Zingerman's
PRESS

Ann Arbor, Michigan

Published in the United States of America by
Zingerman's Press
Manufactured in Michigan, United States of America

First Edition

2012 2011 2010 2009   4 3 2 1

Cover illustrations: Ian Nagy
Cover design and frontmatter: Nicole Robichaud
Text illustrations: Ian Nagy and Ryan Stiner
Text design and layout: Jillian Downey

ISBN-13: 978-0-964-89564-5
ISBN-10: 0-964-89564-1

www.zingermanspress.com

. . . .

Printed, bound and warehoused locally, in southeastern Michigan.

Printed on paper with a recycled content of 30% post-consumer waste.
The recycled content conserved approximately: 20 trees, 14 million BTUs
of energy, 1,770 lbs of CO_2 and 7,350 gallons of water. *Source: Environmental
Defense Fund Paper Calculator.*

. . . .

Contents

The Bacons

Can't wait to get to the meat of the matter?
Skip straight to page 49 and meet the bacons!

Recipes

Hungry? Head to page 153 and start cookin'!

"Nothing is quite as intoxicating as the smell of bacon frying in the morning, save perhaps the smell of coffee brewing."
—James Beard

"Mmm . . . bacon."
—Homer Simpson

Why Bacon?

A whole book about bacon? I don't know. Why not? People's passions for it are running unbelievably high these days. Seriously, the stuff is generating so much energy that it's making Celtics fans at playoff time start to look sedate. Even though I know that people are high on bacon, I'm still blown away by their near-explosive response whenever I bring up the subject. The passion cuts across all ages, ethnic groups and gender lines. I've seen kids get totally wired about it, demanding slice after slice with big smiles on their faces. Even otherwise serious adults get this wide-eyed, lit-up thing, like the look that people at Zingerman's Roadhouse get when one of our donut sundaes is put in front of them. One guy, an engineer, comes into the Roadhouse regularly and orders triple-sized sides (not too well done!) to go with his dinner.

Just the other night I asked a well-traveled American olive oil producer—Joeli Yaguda, who, with her husband and mother-in-law, makes Pasolivo olive oil in central California—what she thinks about bacon. I asked because while working on this book I've taken to asking most everyone. I also happen to like Joeli, and trust her good palate and commitment to good food. She may make olive oil, but it was instantly obvious that her love for bacon knows no bounds. Her eyes opened wide in that way that suggests a level of alertness most high school teachers only dream about. "Oh my god," she gushed. "It's the best! In our family it's the fifth food group. I love it!"

"In my family, bacon is the 5th food group. I love it."
– Joeli Yaguda

Given that bacon contains no caffeine (there's a label claim to make), isn't chocolate, and has little, if any, sugar, I find it somewhat impressive that it elicits such enthusiasm. I'm starting to think there's some as-yet-unknown chemical component in it that stimulates one's pheromones: people go on about it to a degree that seems all out of proportion to what, at its essence, is still just a bit of cured and, more often than not, smoked pork belly. Here at Zingerman's, for example, we're selling tons of bacon burgers, bazillions of BLTs, lots and lots of bacon by the pound, and ever more memberships to our monthly Bacon Club.

Pretty much everybody connected to the food world has got the bacon bug: restaurants are featuring it, chefs-cum-food chemists are making bacon foam, chocolatiers are blending bacon with cacao, consumers are consuming it in ever-greater quantities. Religion and vegetarianism are about the only things that appear to hold anyone back, and even then there are notable exceptions (more about that later). The bottom line is that people get incredibly (insert intensifier of your choosing) pumped up about their bacon. As Bill Marvel of the *Dallas Morning News* wrote, "We are living in the Golden Age of Bacon."

In *Sex and Bacon: Why I Love Things That Are Very, Very Bad for Me*, former sex-worker and current feminist food writer Sarah Katherine Lewis sets out to determine what she calls her "BQ" (bacon quotient). Her goal is to establish her own personal benchmark and to achieve some sense of (perhaps short-lived) satisfaction. Cooking pan after pan of bacon, she discovered her BQ to be a mind-boggling four pounds! While it's fun to read about Lewis' love affair with bacon, I haven't been inspired to investigate my own BQ. I'm happy to just enjoy a bit of good bacon on a regular basis; personally, I have no need to eat an entire week's worth in one sitting, just to prove I can do it.

My reasons for delving into the bacon world don't really have much to do with its present-day popularity or the profusion of publicly proclaimed pork passions. Knowing how these trends go, the popularity of bacon will eventually crash: in July of 2008, *New York Magazine* was already wondering, "When will the anti-bacon backlash come?" Ironically *New York* posed this question on the hundredth birthday of Harriette Simpson Arnow, author of a range of books on the history and people of Kentucky and Tennessee. While bacon may today be riding the ups and downs of a modern media craze, Arnow demonstrates that it was already extremely popular in seventeenth-century Tennessee and Kentucky. In fact, present mania aside, we've been eating bacon in large quantities for thousands of years, and it seems likely that we're going to be eating it for many more to come.

What fascinates me about bacon isn't the latest trends but old-time taste, tradition and technique . . . and the people who make it all happen. I want to understand the bacon world of the past, to get a better sense of where today's bacon comes from, and to help people understand how they can bring bacon into their everyday cooking and eating. So back to my original question—why bother putting together an entire book about bacon? Because writing does for my intellectual and emotional appreciation of bacon what a hot frying pan does for "pig"—it takes the soft, almost nondescript raw material and makes it all come alive. The bacon basics—what bacon is and how to cook it—are really pretty darned simple. But drop a few slices in a hot skillet and suddenly everything comes together. The smell, the sizzle, the texture, the sheen, the sensuality, the feel all come forward in ways that you just wouldn't predict from looking at those slack pink-and-white slices. For me, at least (and I hope for you too, since you're sitting and reading all this), the writing, like the hot pan, brings out all the other stuff that makes the subject matter so special. It connects me with the people and the product in ever livelier and more meaningful ways.

Having worked on this book for many months now, I now have a sense that there's so much more to bacon than I realized when I started: it's about the history, the people, the craft, its many uses, and how incredibly, wildly wound up people get about it.

Joeli Yaguda, the pork-loving olive oil producer, told me that, "Bacon has always been something I love. But—like single-malt scotch—it's much more fun when your passion is shared with someone else." She recalls that when she met her husband Josh and realized that his (Jewish) mother could eat a pound of bacon at a sitting, she felt right at home. I hope you feel at home here as well, and that you enjoy some of the flavor of the great bacons and incredible people I've gotten to know while writing this book.

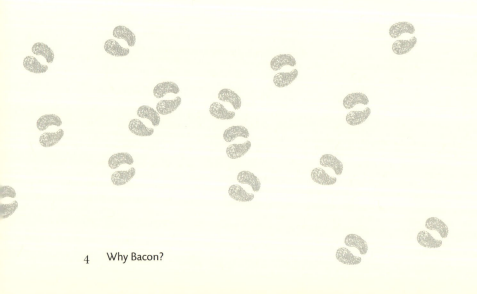

Big Bacon Learning Objectives

After many years of designing training workshops with Maggie Bayless, managing partner at ZingTrain (Zingerman's training and organizational change business), the need to establish clear learning objectives up front has pretty much been branded into my brain. If I'm going to ask you to read an entire book on bacon, I'd better be clear on what we're hoping to achieve. So, by the time you finish this book, you will:

1. Have heard a whole lot more about the history and handling of bacon than you'd have ever imagined there was to know.

2. Be able to pass the official bacon Trivia Test at the end of this book with flying colors.

3. Be able to tell anyone who asks what your four favorite bacons are and have a list of others you're ready to try.

4. Be ready to go out and prepare any of the bacon-based recipes at the back of the book.

Well? Are you in? Let's get started with a little trip to Camp Bacon.

When the Southern Foodways Alliance—my favorite food-based educational nonprofit by a mile—sponsored a field trip to Louisville a few years ago, they called it "Camp Bacon." I really wanted to be there, but I just couldn't swing the schedule stuff to make it happen. Not being a bacon-only specialist I had other food activities on my plate—I'd already committed to attending Slow Food's biennial "Cheese" festival in northern Italy (I know, it's a rough job . . .). But while I didn't get to Kentucky to take part in the bacon festivities, the name "Camp Bacon" has stuck in my head ever since.

There's just something about the idea of Camp Bacon that conjures up great images. Bacon on the bonfire—chunks of it speared on pointed wooden sticks, held over an open fire until the outside edges are dark and crispy, then letting the fat drip onto bread or vegetables. Blue jeans and black hooded Camp Bacon sweatshirts with shredded cuffs, smelling like sweetly smoked pork belly. Bacon competitions—not eating contests, which strike me as needless excess—but maybe classes in bacon cooking and slicing, bacon-sack races, bacon-sack puppet shows, bacon 'n' marshmallow s'mores, songs like Andre Williams' "Bacon Fat" in guitar-strumming sing-a-longs, bacon-making merit badges . . . I can sense the buzz building already. Wait until *New York Magazine* gets hold of this one!

Of course, even if there'd been a Camp Bacon when I was a kid, I'd never have been allowed to get near the place. Growing up in a kosher home, bacon was way out of bounds. While we ate meat in restaurants, pork was always completely *not* OK. Warnings and admonitions were unnecessary: not eating pork was as given as a given could be. And because we didn't hang out with—nor, I guess, really even eat meals with—non-Jewish people, I truly think I had no sense of what bacon was about. I suppose I must have seen it on TV or read about it in books. (Did the Hardy Boys eat bacon for breakfast? Back then food wasn't particularly high on my list of passions, so even though I probably read every book in the series, I couldn't really tell you.)

At home, in our observant Jewish kitchen, the closest we ever came was "kosher beef bacon," which, if you haven't had it, bears some resemblance to bacon in appearance but almost none when it comes to flavor. It's a barely remarkable little footnote to food history—I can't remember anyone ever talking about the stuff with the kind of energy inspired by the properly porcine original. I suppose it's like being served a spoonful of enticing-but-not-too-tasty Cool Whip (which I also grew up on) instead of real whipped cream. Mind you, I'm not saying that my bacon-deprived childhood was cause to put anyone away for child abuse or anything. Beef bacon was (and I guess still probably is) perfectly edible. Which, sadly, means that unlike Tang, Space Sticks or any of those other silly foodstuffs people of my generation grew up on, it wasn't even bad enough to rise to the level of kitsch.

When it finally came time for me to try bacon, I think I was actually a little bit afraid. Stuff that's taboo . . . for me, life isn't a race into new territory. I think too much. I'm sure I didn't tell anyone that I'd never had it. I probably just went off to the side of wherever I was and snuck a taste when no one was looking. And I'm sure I liked it well enough. But, in honesty, it wasn't a love at first bite sort of thing. For me, the romance with bacon was more gradual. But, as in real romance, I think this actually led to a more stable and long-lasting relationship.

I do remember that my favorite breakfasts when I was working as an early-morning line cook were these little BLTs that we made on onion rolls. It was before we opened Zingerman's Deli and I was working in other people's restaurants, so the bacon wasn't particularly good. Even so, the sandwiches were pretty tasty, and making them now with better bread and better bacon they're a fine way to get your day going. Fresh onion rolls (I use what the Zingerman's Bakehouse folks call New Yorkers: soft little white rolls stuffed with a pocketful of toasted onion bits and poppy seeds), lots of mayo, hot slices of just-cooked bacon, and, of course, lettuce and tomato. The coolness of the vegetables against the heat of the bacon is great. It's one of those sandwiches that you can squish down in your fist to eat one-handed, so that the mayo and the bacon fat really get into the bread.

In truth, I probably started my digging into bacon's background with more than a Tiddly Wink's worth of skepticism. But my wariness has been worn down: the more I'm around bacon, the more interested I get, and the more I like to cook with it. I use it with fish, sprinkle it on salads, sauté it up with vegetables, add it to cornmeal mush and eat it with eggs. Of course it goes well with grits, pastas, stews and soups, too, and I use bits of it in all of them with increasing regularity. Fortunately, you don't need a lot to make a difference. In truth, I rarely make bacon the star of the show, but it's definitely appearing in the cast with ever-greater frequency.

Now, all that being said, you shouldn't let my own moderate tendencies interfere with your passion for smoked and cured pork bellies. To the contrary, as a writer and a foodseller it's in my interest—financial, intellectual and emotional—to feed your bacon love, to whip you into a big bacon-buying frenzy. So do it! Read up. Eat up. Build the passion. Buy bacon. Cook bacon. Love bacon. Everything will be better . . .

Bacon for President

If you asked me to name a single ingredient, the availability, under-standing and use of which changed American cooking in the 1990s more than any other, I'd quickly point to olive oil. Although 20 years ago most Americans certainly knew what olive oil was, hardly anyone not of Mediterranean origin had tried anything except the bland, low-end commercial versions. But as better oils became available and Americans embraced Mediterranean cooking, olive oil—*good* olive oil!—found its way into millions of the nation's kitch-ens. And it didn't just sit there looking good, either. People really learned to use the stuff.

Similarly, if you were to ask me what single ingredient is going to alter American cooking in the next decade, I'd put big bucks on bacon. Like olive oil, everyone's heard of it, and almost everyone's eaten it. But the bacon most folks have had is little better than the commercial olive oil we were served for so long. Which means that most people really haven't experienced just how good bacon can be.

It's hardly newsworthy anymore to claim that "everything's better with bacon." But the thing is, unlike the typical marketing malarkey, this catchphrase seems to hold true. Bacon works with salads and sandwiches, shrimp, shad, steaks and scallops. Tomatoes for sure. The Bakehouse's Bacon Farm Bread has attracted a very large cult following. Cornmeal and cauliflower are both enhanced by a bit of bacon. You could easily build a whole book on the subject of BLTs. Pork loin is . . . already pork, but it's even better when you lay some bacon on it while it's roasting (which I suppose is the porcine equiv-alent of the very delicious act of dressing olives with additional olive oil). Bacon even works in desserts: apple crisp with bacon and but-termilk biscuits served with chocolate (and bacon) gravy are both pretty darned good ways to end a meal. In fact, I've included recipes for both at the end of this book.

A Bit of Bacon History

Although it's getting hampersful of headlines these days, bacon has almost always been around. In his I'm sure not-best-selling 1917 book, *Bacon and Hams*, George J. Nicholls writes that, "All men have an interest in bacon, with the exception, perhaps, of the Jew; and the man of little imagination, but of sound appetitive instincts, who had bacon and eggs for breakfast one morning, and varied the monotony by ordering eggs and bacon the next, was more than justified by almost unanimous vote of the community—the pig is the true autocrat of the breakfast table." Nor is the passionate use of pork fat as a "secret" ingredient new, either. In his autobiography, *A Chef's Tale*, Pierre Franey wrote of his early twentieth-century childhood that, "One of my mother's favorite tricks was to render pork fat until only the crackling was left and mix in that crackling with her bread dough, the result being a familiar French bread with crunchy surprises all the way through; it was almost like finding almonds embedded in chocolate."

Humans have probably been eating cured pork in one form or another for an awfully long time. Wild boars have been around for about 40,000 years and the domesticated hogs we know and love to eat today date back about 7,000 years, to China. From Asia, pigs were brought to the Middle East and then on to Europe, where pork soon became a favorite food of the Greeks and the Romans. Hogs are a relatively recent addition to North American eating, however: the first of them likely set foot in Florida with the Hernando de Soto expedition in 1539. While they're not as prolific as rabbits, pigs breed quickly and raising them doesn't take a whole lot of work. Wherever they were raised, their propensity for rapid weight gain made them entrepreneurially appealing, as well as culinarily compelling.

Like most everyone else around, I'd probably encountered the phrase "bring home the bacon" hundreds of times without ever really knowing where it came from. It turns out that it dates back to 1104 and the English town of Little Dunmow in Essex, in the southeastern corner of England. It lies about 25 miles inland from two of my favorite food towns: Tiptree, where the famous jams and jellies come from, and Maldon, where they make the classic English sea salt. Apparently Dunmow's Lord of the Manor and his wife dressed as country folk and called on the local prior, asking for his blessing to mark a year and a day since they'd been happily married. Despite their humble appearance, the Prior not only gave the couple his blessing but also offered them a side of bacon. The Lord revealed his true identity and, in appreciation of the Prior's generosity, returned the favor by promising a side of bacon—known in Old English as a "flitch"—to any couple who could prove a year and a day's worth of wedded peace and happiness. A husband who "brought home the bacon" was thus held in high esteem for his upstanding behavior. For centuries, couples traveled to Little Dunmow to make their case in the hope of being awarded a flitch of their own.

The "Flitch Trials" fell off in the early eighteenth century, but they were reintroduced sometime thereafter at the behest of Harrison Ainsworth, author of the 1854 novel *The Flitch of Bacon, or, the Custom of Dunmow.* Much to my surprise, the tradition continues to this day. The Trials are now held every leap year. In a scene that we might want to reenact at Camp Bacon, couples present evidence to the village court that they haven't quarreled nor ever even thought of getting out of their marriage over the previous 366 days (or 367 days during leap years). In July of 2008, four couples—three English and one American—successfully "brought home the bacon." While you won't see their names on page one of your hometown paper, you can find them at http://www.dunmowflitchtrials.co.uk/.

In colonial America, the traditions of pork curing arrived soon after the first European settlers. Bacon provided sustenance in a difficult setting. Regardless of how well a colonial-era couple got

Sing a Streaky Song

While you're immersing yourself in baconology, why not check out the song "Streak o' Lean, Streak o' Fat," recently recorded by the band Uncle Earl on their *Waterloo, Tennessee* CD. They have Ann Arbor and, actually, Zingerman's roots! The music itself is a traditional fast-paced American fiddle tune, originally titled "Hell Broke Loose in Georgia," then recorded under the current title by A. A. Gray (that's "Ahaz August," in case you were wondering) of Carroll County, Georgia.

The words on the modern-day Uncle Earl version are new, written by band member Abigail Washburn with friend Jon Campbell and Kang Mao, the lead singer of a Beijing hardcore punk band called The Subs. Abigail lived in China when she was in college, and the lyrics are a combination of the traditional English and Abby's newly added Chinese. The latter part of the song refers to *hongshao rou,* which is apparently thought to have been Mao Zedong's favorite dish from his home province of Hunan. Abby describes it in the liner notes as "composed of a small streak of lean meat with a big hunk of fat." "It freaks out the foreigners when it lands on the dinner table," she says. "If desired, a correlation could be drawn between the nutritional makeup of hongshao rou and the efficacy of general governance during the Chinese Cultural Revolution."

To take the excitement up a notch still further, the "g'Earls" from Uncle Earl report that they've taken to doing the song as an audience participation number. Abigail yells out "hongshao rou" and the crowd responds with a loud cry of "BACON!" To quote bandmate KC Groves, who used to frequent the Deli when she lived in Ann Arbor, "Oh, the power of having a few thousand people yelling 'Bacon' at you!!! " I love it. Good music, strange historical references and bacon all blending into track #10 on this really fine, bluegrass-based and John Paul Jones-produced CD. For me, the fiddle work alone makes me want to fry up some fatback and have some serious culinary fun.

on in their marriage, bacon could be brought home . . . and kept
there, because of its long shelf life. Hogs have been a key element of
American agriculture, eating and economics ever since. American
bacon and ham were exported back to England alongside peanuts
and tobacco as early as 1639. By the end of the seventeenth century
the average American farmer had four or five hogs, which he used
primarily to feed his family and also a bit for trade. Bacon became a
culinary common denominator: most every ethnic group relied on
it. Even Native Americans, who'd clearly never eaten it before the
sixteenth century, quickly adopted it.

Pork was very much the premier product of the American
countryside—up until about 1850 it made up a greater percentage
of American eating than every other foodstuff combined, except
wheat. Bacon was used in all sorts of dishes: with vegetables or
beans, in soups and on salads, in the form of meat or as a fat used in
the traditional boiled dressing for the warm salad typical of colonial
times. In areas where hogs were raised, they were very much woven
into the seasonal cycles of life. Pigs would be allowed to run in the
woods or fields through the summer and autumn and then slaughtered late in the fall, when cold weather came and the forests ran
out of food. In the mountain areas that meant that many hogs had
the chance to feed on acorns, chestnuts or hickory nuts. In more
agricultural areas, they'd likely have finished up in the fields eating
the leavings after the main crops had been collected. In either case,
these final weeks of feeding naturally improved both the flavor of
the meat and its healthfulness.

The slaughter typically took place sometime around Christmas
or New Year's, depending on the local weather. I can't really explain
the science of it, but a lot of lore warns that you should only slaughter when the moon is full or nearly so. In the *Foxfire Book*, a classic
collection of Appalachian folk knowledge, one person advises that,
"You got t'kill it on th'right time of the moon. You don't never want
to kill on th' new moon." Another says, "We'd kill hogs on th'full
moon, or just about th'full moon. While th'moon was shrinkin',

Call of the Wild

As pigs became commonplace in colonial America, some naturally escaped the farm and went feral. Said to have been exceptionally ugly and exceedingly tough, these "wood hogs" were prevalent anywhere where pigs were raised. As late as the 1960s, *The Foxfire Book* reports, "hogs were hunted, like bears, with specially trained dogs." The hunter would take hold of the hog's ear "and get as close to its side as he could to stay out of danger . . . Then the hunter would lasso the hog, put one rope on his front leg and one on his back, and lead him out." It wasn't a risk-free activity—a cornered hog could do a lot of damage.

These wild pigs acquired an array of great slang names. Charles Wayland Towne and Edward Norris Wentworth list a few in their book, *Pigs, from Cave to Corn Belt:* acorn gatherer, bristle bearer, wood wanderer, wound maker, mountain liver, alligator, landpike, prairie racer, stump rooter, hazelnut splitter and razorback.

If we have a Zingerman's football team one day, I don't think I'd mind calling them the Hazelnut Splitters.

the meat'd shrink. There'd be a lot a lard an' grease if it'uz on th'shrinkin' of th'moon. If it wus on th' new moon, you wouldn't make much lard, and th'meat'd swell up when y'cooked it 'stead'a shrink. Other farmers would kill their own hogs when the moon was shrinking, but they would take hogs to market when the moon was growing so that the meat would weigh more." The same idea took root in Ireland, among other places: In *Land of Milk and Honey*, Brid Mahon wrote that, "In the counties of Mayo and Galway it was believed that the killing should take place under a full moon. If the animal was killed when the moon was waning, the meat would reduce in size, while if the killing was done when the moon was waxing or full the meat would increase."

Once the slaughter was over, many farm families would enjoy fresh pork for a couple of weeks. Most of the animal, though, was made into sausages, hams and bacon. Fresh sausages were eaten early on, then the smaller cured ones. Among families of Middle European or Mediterranean origin, the larger, hard-cured salamis might be ready in late spring. Cured country hams came last, starting in the fall and hopefully lasting all the way up until the next slaughter.

Bacon really had no season. Unlike the hams, it was ready to eat a matter of weeks after slaughter. And heavily smoked and/or cured, it could be kept all the way through the year. In *Seedtime on the Cumberland*, Harriette Arnow reports that having bacon and ham on hand was considered a "symbol of the good life": for a family to still have bacon or ham in the smokehouse when the next season's meats were being put up to cure was a sure sign of economic success.

As Americans moved westward into "unsettled" territory ("the West" back then was what we'd now call the eastern Midwest), they took their hogs with them. By 1840 the four and a half million people who lived in the seven states bounded by Pennsylvania to the east, Mississippi to the south and west, and Tennessee to the north owned a total of ten million hogs. Tennessee's pig population of three million was the biggest in the U.S., with Kentucky a close second. (It's not a big surprise then that those became two of the biggest bacon- and country ham-producing states.) While early slaughtering was concentrated on the East Coast, by the middle of the nineteenth century the center of the industry had moved to Cincinnati, which became known as "Porkopolis."

In those years of land claims and long-distance wagon routes, bacon was a staple on most every trip. The standard provisions for cross-country travel most often included flour, sugar, lard, beans, dried fruit, salt, pepper and, of course, a LOT of bacon—it was common to stock 100 to 150 pounds per person. Bacon was also given out in large quantities for Army cooking, where its long shelf life, high protein content and full flavor made it a reliable fallback for feeding hungry soldiers in less-than-ideal circumstances. In fact, bacon was such a big part of Civil War cookery that some folks speculated the Army was trying to feed the troops solely on flour and bacon. Soldiers commonly prepared a dish called "cornmeal cush": bacon was fried up in a skillet, a bit of water was added to make a brown gravy, and then cornmeal was cooked in to thicken the dish into a filling porridge. Others made "skillygalee": hardtack biscuits that were first soaked in water and then fried in pork or bacon fat (essentially an American version of the Iberian bread-and-pork-fat dish called *migas*). More on this point in a minute, but note the prominence of bacon and the way it was used to flavor most everything else, much as olive oil has been in the Mediterranean for so many centuries.

What is Bacon, Anyway?

Well, I *thought* that was a pretty simple question. But bacon, like most things in life, turned out to be more complicated than I'd originally anticipated. Up until the latter part of the sixteenth century, bacon (or "bacoun") was a Middle English word that people used to refer to pork of any sort. The term is likely taken from the French *bako*, Common Germanic *bakkon* and Old Teutonic *backe*, all of which refer to the "back," the part of the pig typically used for bacon-making in Europe.

Interestingly, and oddly, bacon as we know it over here in the U.S. comes not from the back but from the belly and side of the pig. That seems to be an anatomical disconnect until you realize that in

Europe the term "bacon" means something entirely different than it does over here. William Tullberg, whom I know from his work with Wiltshire Tracklements, an excellent line of British mustards and condiments, actually started his career working with the Harris family, who are responsible for the now well-known (in Britain, not here) Wiltshire Cure bacon. Tullberg explained that the belly is not where it's at in the British bacon world. "An Englishman (even a quarter Swedish one, like me)," he writes, "thinks of bacon in terms of a whole cured Wiltshire side, gammon, back, streak, and shoulder. Asking for 'bacon' in a shop, he would expect to be offered sliced back or streak, smoked or green. The gammon is sold either as a joint to be cooked as ham, or sliced as gammon rashers, and the shoulder is sold as a joint, and when cooked, is often referred to as 'shoulder ham.'"

While I'm sure that that explanation makes perfect sense to William, he had me completely lost before he even finished the second sentence. I was wandering the British outskirts of Camp Bacon, with neither a compass nor a British-American dictionary to guide me. I'd heard the word "gammon" a million times, but I had no idea what one actually was. Fortunately, William was willing to assist, so . . . with his help and a couple of successful keyword searches I quickly learned that the term comes from old French, and refers to the rear leg of the pig. It was apparently used centuries ago to describe whole sides of pork, including both the back and the belly. Today, gammon is generally defined more narrowly to mean a ham: hence, a "gammon steak" is a ham steak. And "green" means cured but not smoked.

It's not easy being green . . . or at least it's not so easy to understand what all this is about. As William said, "I've seen many a mystified Englishman unable to understand that bacon in America means cured belly pork, complaining bitterly that his breakfast bacon and eggs was not right, because he expected sliced back bacon!" Maynard, the one-named British author of one of my favorite books about bacon, *Adventures of a Bacon Curer*, confirms the con-

Bacon Down Under

Lance Corporal Bacon is basically a block of pork fat with a small streak of pork meat. It got its name during WWI from Australian and New Zealand Army Corps troops, who were regularly served it as part of their rations. The name was bestowed because the thin strip of meat in this low-end, made-for-the-military pork belly echoed the single stripe on a lance corporal's sleeve. Very witty, those Australians.

fusion. (Since you'll be seeing his name many times as you read, I should mention that it's pronounced in a sort of Anglicized French as "may-NARD," with the emphasis mostly, though not fully, on the second syllable, rather than the way I grew up with here, which is more like "MAY-nerd.") In recounting the story of his first trip to the U.S.—a visit with a bacon-making Pennsylvania Amish farm family—he writes that, "I thought it was a lovely bacon." It was "streaky," he explains, and not the sort that he was used to making in Britain, which would have been cured loin. The latter, he adds, "was not cured, they eat the loin as [fresh] pork."

The terminology clearly causes confusion. So hopefully the following glossary will help English visitors avoid embarrassment in the U.S., and Americans avoid any gaffes in the UK.

Bacon Glossary

Bacon: Over here in the U.S., cured and usually, though not always, smoked pork belly.

British Bacon: Today, this generally refers to the back and not the belly, cured in a brine solution but not smoked.

Canadian Peameal Bacon: Pork loin cured in a wet brine solution and then rolled in cornmeal. The real thing is sold raw and never smoked.

Dry Cure (a.k.a. *Country Cure*): Raw pork rubbed and then set into a dry solution of salt, sugar and spices (instead of a brine) to cure the pork before it's smoked.

Fatback: The strip of fat from the top of the hog's back, above the loin. Used extensively in old-style American cooking, it really has no meat on it whatsoever. In the South you'll still see places selling fried fatback. Typically used to make lard and cracklins.

Flitch: The old English word for a side of bacon.

Green: The British term for cured but unsmoked bacon.

Guanciale: Italian-style pork jowl, dry-cured and unsmoked.

Irish Bacon: Same as British bacon, but often used for boiling.

Lardo: Italian-style pork back fat, dry-cured in slabs for months. Sliced and eaten raw.

Long Back or Long Middle: Used in England to describe bacon sold as loin with belly still attached.

Pancetta: Dry-cured but unsmoked Italian-style bacon made from pork belly.

Rashers: Slices of bacon, to a Brit.

Streak o' Lean: Like fatback, but with (at most) a small strip of meat in it. Michael Stern, writing in *Roadfood*, says, "streak o' lean provides maximum piggy flavor. If you never can get enough bacon, it's the breakfast meat for you." Sometimes smoked, sometimes not. Also like fatback, streak o' lean can be floured and deep-fried to make a crisp little bacony snack.

Streaky Bacon: What British people ask for when they want American-style belly bacon.

Wet Cure: Bacon that spends a good bit of time in a saltwater brine, most often, though not always, with sugar and spices.

Wide: The wide side of the pork loin as it's used for bacon—it's from further up the top loin, toward the shoulder.

Where Have All the Drovers Gone?

Sorry, I can't resist the subtitle—the tune slipped into my head while I was out running one day, and I couldn't get it out. So . . . if Peter, Paul and Mary had lived in the second half of the nineteenth century instead of the twentieth, their big hit could well have been, "Where Have All the Drovers Gone?" While you most certainly won't see any such openings on Craig's List, thousands of Americans once worked as drovers, the less glamorous (but probably more important) eighteenth-century piggy equivalent of cowboys like Rowdy Yates and Gil Favor from *Rawhide.*

In one of those interesting, now all-but-forgotten footnotes of history there was once an entire profession having to do with pork that's completely lost to us today. It's a line of work I certainly would never have thought about, had I not come across it while doing some reading on nineteenth-century American agriculture. But once you read about drovers, the need for them seems obvious: in order for urban dwellers to get fresh pork to eat, pigs had to be brought from the farms on which they were raised in the rural areas of North America to the cities where they could be slaughtered, sold and served. Before the introduction of the railroads, there was really only one practical way to do so: the hogs had to walk. And since the very valuable pigs weren't going to be allowed to make the trip un-chaperoned, they were shepherded along their routes by men known as "drovers." Without the drovers there would have been no American pork industry. Bacon would have been forever limited to on-the-family-farm consumption.

While I'm sure others were at it in less recognizable places, the first formal record of North American drovers that I've found concerns William and John Pynchon. The Pynchon brothers started taking livestock from Springfield, Massachusetts, into Boston in 1655. By the end of the seventeenth century theirs had become a well-accepted profession. Farmers driving their own hogs generally had an easier time of it because the animals were comfortable with them. But more often, professional drovers went around the countryside buying a few hogs from each farmer they encountered (most farmers had only four or five pigs, one or two of which were typically to be kept for the family) and gradually gathering them up into a single, large herd. While the boss might ride a horse or wagon, most men walked their way through the hog drives.

Long-distance driving began in 1800 and probably reached its peak by about 1825. A long drive in those days could take three

months—the herd made five to ten miles a day if they were doing well. To keep them moving effectively, domesticated pigs were trained to respond to the blowing of a conch shell. En route, drovers risked theft, porcine illness and bad weather: thunderstorms could cause the hogs to panic and stampede. And even under the best of circumstances weight loss was always an issue: pigs often dropped ten to twelve pounds during a drive (I'd guess the drovers lost some weight, as well).

A whole industry grew up around the drives. Drovers had to pay tolls on each hog whenever they traveled on a turnpike (in 1817 the Philadelphia-Pittsburgh route charged a toll of six cents per 20 hogs). A well-positioned stock stand on the turnpike might see a few hundred thousand pigs pass through in a year. The biggest season for driving was late fall, just before slaughtering time. Spring was popular as well, whereas summer heat and winter cold made the long cross-country walks almost impossibly difficult in those seasons. Innkeepers along the route were often paid in lame hogs, which could be turned into provisions for the table. Nor was droving an exclusively American occupation: a great tradition of bacon-making sprang up around Wiltshire, England, in part because the area was a resting point for drovers moving Irish pigs from the port of Bristol up to London.

The demand for drovers—here, in Britain, and probably everywhere else—began to drop off as the railroads came to dominate commercial transportation in the second half of the nineteenth century. Not surprisingly there was a great deal of opposition to the railroads along the driving routes. As you already know, the railroads won out and the drovers disappeared—as did other once-essential and now-unneeded occupations like ice-harvesting and stagecoach driving. The only modern reference I've ever seen to drovers is the name of a Chicago-based band.

Death of a Slaughterman

In *Adventures of a Bacon Curer,* Maynard mentions another no-longer-existent, pig-related profession: the journeyman-curer. In early twentieth-century England this was a man who "would come down and kill the pig. He would stop overnight and cure the pig the next day, and that was the ritual. It was important that he did it correctly as that was the main meat source for the winter." In her *Irish Traditional Cooking,* Darina Allen describes a similar scene: ". . . on my relative's farm in Tipperary," she writes, "a local man skilled in the killing of pigs would arrive on an ass's cart, bringing all the tools of his trade—a mallet, a knife, a saw, an apron and a galvanized bath. He was highly thought of and had to be booked ahead." I can't say that these journeymen have disappeared entirely, but I've not (yet!) heard tell of one still in business.

No one I've asked in the U.S. remembers such curers here. The closest I came was in a story from bacon-maker extraordinaire Allan Benton: "In the hills of Virginia it was common to have someone in the community who would go around at hog butchering time and help the neighbors slaughter the hogs and help work up the meat. They were usually paid either with money or in fresh pork."

Back in Britain, Maynard writes that there are quite a few stories about the old journeymen-curers and how they were compensated. "Sometimes they were paid in surprising ways," he writes. "And sometimes," he goes on, "they left a few children behind."

Modern-Day Droving

Interestingly, this all plays into the connection—and then discon-
nection—between the quality of our pork and changes in the way
the supply chain worked. It's really not much different from the
commercial corn cultivation that Michael Pollan wrote about in
The Omnivore's Dilemma. When farm families raised a hog or two for
their own consumption, there was a high interest in attention to
detail. Since the people who raised the pigs also ate the bacon, ham
and fresh pork, the farmer had every incentive to improve the eating quality of the meat. Farmers generally got along well with their
pigs, the animals' stress level was lower, and the pork they yielded
was likely to have tasted better, since stressed animals produce poor-
quality meat.

As pork "production" became a way to make extra money and
not just feed the family, the advent of drovers begat a gradual loss
of the farmer's incentive to raise the best pork possible. Since his
family wasn't going to eat the end product anyway, quality came to
be defined by weight gain, not flavor. Today, the separation between
pig and production has grown even wider. It plays hard, I think, into
the issue of pork quality, and also into the use of CAFOs (Concentrated Animal Feeding Operations).

With that background in mind, I figured I'd start my digging
into what makes for better bacon by talking with a man who's spent
a lifetime raising pigs. Paul Willis is the guy who started the Niman
Ranch pork program back in 1995, and has grown it from the
confines of his own place in Thornton, Iowa, to a network of over
500 family hog farmers all over his own state (and of late into a few
other spots in the Midwest, as well). Paul is, flat out, as passionate
about traditional hog-rearing as anyone I've ever met. And although
he's as quiet and Iowa-considerate as anyone could be, his passion
comes through in everything he says.

Paul started out with a little lesson on the value of good feed and
good breed. "The [modern] pigs are so lean you can hardly make

bacon out of them," he began. "I think there's an opinion out there that if you have a processed product like bacon, you can get by with using any old thing. And, you know, I just don't think that's true. It may be that the differences are more subtle, but they're still there. It's just what I think to be true. I don't have a lot of tests. If nothing else, I feel better about our (Niman Ranch) bacon because of the quality of the fresh pork. We get tons of compliments about our bacon."

That was the soft intro. Where he really went off was on the CAFOs, the hog farming counterpart of the cages in which commercial chickens are now kept. "I guess my feelings on bacon are, like on anything else, you have to start out with good raw material. And it seems like pork bellies without the smell of hog confinement pit gasses are probably preferable."

Paul's description is poignant, but most of us only encounter pigs in the form of processed pork. We don't see or smell the hogs. They do in Iowa, though. "I don't know if people who aren't around it realize what it's like," Paul said. "We've got a neighbor putting up a building to house six thousand hogs. We're not happy about it. It further divides the community. These people don't have any idea what they're doing and they're thinking that they're going to get free manure. But the smell can be so bad that people who live nearby can't even stand outside. You know it's gotten to the point if I go by and smell that smell it almost instantly gives me a headache."

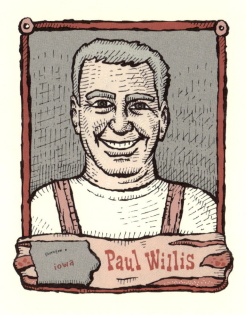

Having been to Iowa and the Willis' farm in person, I can vouch for what he's saying: well-cared-for hogs that are allowed to move around freely in the fields don't stink; they're healthy and healthful and they're part of the farm community. And, as Paul said, it just makes sense that the bacon would taste better as a result.

The Olive Oil of North America

I know it sounds a little strange at first. But seriously, I've come to believe ever more ardently that bacon is to North American cooking and culture very much what olive oil is to the people of the Mediterranean. Dismiss the idea as oddball theory if you want; I know I did, the first time it came to my mind. But the more I think about it, the more the idea makes sense. Yeah, I know the analogy's probably not perfect. For openers, any food history fan can tell you that, while olive oil's been in the Mediterranean since time immemorial, hogs only arrived in the New World with the conquistadors, about 40 years after Columbus. Still, the more I mull it over, the more reading and cooking I do, the more people I talk to, the more there seems to be something to the comparison.

The validity of the idea was confirmed for me one night while I was making cornmeal mush. In the traditional recipe, the mush is served with nothing more than fried pieces of bacon and a lot of bacon fat. Does polenta with olive oil sound good? Well, then why not cornmeal mush with bacon fat? The former sounds Euro-glamorous, the latter like redneck fare, but the mush is equally, marvelously delicious. So, yeah, I'm going with my theory.

Here we go—ten solid reasons why bacon is the olive oil of North America:

1. *People really, really love the stuff*

When it comes to social and/or culinary change, I can tell you from experience: passion counts for a lot. In the Mediterranean, olive oil is something most every good cook cares deeply about. Unlike coffee in, say, Colombia, olive oil is not an imported crop that's grown mostly for economic gain. People in every part of the Mediterranean really *love* their olive oil, and they eat a lot of it. They have strong feelings about it. They get excited about using it.

Bacon is about as close as it gets to that same passion in North American eating. I can't think of any other ingredient that generates such commotion here. Seriously, you start talking bacon to people and they go hog-wild. People who cook, sure, but also those who just like to eat: professionals or home cooks, older folks and kids, they all love bacon. It gets them excited. Their eyes light up. They share recipes. They tell stories. They believe in bacon. And they consume it in very large quantities!

2. *Longstanding, historically sound sustenance*

Given their long histories, I was thinking of writing that neither olive oil nor bacon was "a flash in the pan." But the truth is that nothing flashes quicker than a bit of fat slopped over the edge of a hot sauté pan. In all seriousness, though, while both bacon and olive oil may be getting good press these days, neither one is a passing fad. Olive oil's been a part of Mediterranean culture for thousands of years. Pigs have only been in North America for five hundred, so we're running a bit behind, but bacon has been big here since almost the moment it arrived. Every early American cookbook talks about bacon. Author William Byrd wrote of North Carolinians in the seventeenth century that they ate "pork upon pork and pork again upon that." And most every traveler's tale mentions bacon as one of a dozen key provisions to have on board their boat or wagon.

3. Cutting across political and ethnic boundaries

The love of olive oil and bacon doesn't stop at geopolitical boundaries. Olive trees have outlasted empires (Greeks, Turks, Byzantines and Ottomans). Their fruit and its essence have been common to cuisines of peoples that have been enemies for ages (Greeks and Turks, Israelis and Palestinians), as well as the cookery of regions like Provence that have been dragged back and forth among sovereign states (France, Italy and later France again).

In studying traditional American cooking it's increasingly clear to me that bacon could be our single most historically important ingredient. Like olive oil, which serves as a culinary thread (maybe rope would be a better metaphor) binding together the varied cuisines of the Mediterranean, bacon is the common ingredient of nearly every element of regional American cooking. Anywhere you go they use it, and typically in profusion. You'll certainly find it all over the South, but the Union Army counted on it heavily during the Civil War, too. Bacon has always been big in New England: with clams in chowder, with beans for baking, with eggs for breakfast, for sautéing scallops and dozens of other old-time dishes. The Pennsylvania Dutch use a lot of it in eggs and plenty more in potato salads. And Frederick Law Olmstead wrote in 1856 that, "The universal food of the people of Texas, both rich and poor, seems to be corn-dodgers and fried bacon." Out West I've had bacon with fish and in salads and on sandwiches. And of course north of the border Canadians have loved their unique form of bacon for a long time.

Although, as I've mentioned, it wasn't part of their pre-Columbian cooking tradition, many Native Americans have been using bacon for centuries. Bacon with wild rice is definitely a staple: the fact that bacon came to be so closely connected to—and so often cooked with—the most highly valued and esteemed food among the Native American cultures of the Upper Midwest speaks volumes to its culinary value. Meg Noori, a member of the Ojibway tribe and an expert on their language and traditional storytelling ways, told me, "You have to have bacon in rice. Of course, if it was just us eating you wouldn't get it. But if company was coming . . ."

Meg tells me that macaroni and bacon is a very popular dish among members of her tribe. While the idea may strike you as odd, the idea of pasta tossed with bacon fat and bacon pieces seems very much akin to a simple Mediterranean meal of pasta cooked and tossed with good olive oil. In the latter context, take note, too, that Meg suggested adding chunks of ripe tomato to the pan at the very end, just before plating.

Michael Witgen, a professor of American culture at Michigan and, like Meg, of Ojibway origin, recalls, "My mom cooked with bacon fat all the time until I was 16. Those were good days. The first time my wife came over I threw down a slab of bacon fat and started cooking with it, and she looked at me like I was crazy and said, 'What's that?'"

Michael, Meg and Phil Deloria (the third member in this trio of Native American professors at Michigan) all talked to me about cooking eggs in bacon fat, too: first you cook the bacon, then heat the eggs in the leftover fat, then you fry some bread in the pan. It's basically a three-course, bacon-centered breakfast.

4. The fat is where the flavor is

The flavor of any cuisine, whether you're in Spain or the American South, is carried through the cooking more by the fat than by anything else. I learned long ago that if you want to replicate the traditional flavors of any cuisine you always start by using the right fat. Just like olive oil is the flavor underlying so much Mediterranean food, bacon quietly but forcefully buttresses the flavors of food all over this country. I can't even think of how many folks have told me that adding a bit of bacon fat to whatever they're cooking makes all the difference. John T. Edge, writer, culinary historian and cultural commentator par excellence, who grew up in Georgia, told me that his mother always kept a Dundee jam jar of the stuff next to the stove. "She started every dish with a glug of bacon fat," he said. Down in Atlanta, award-winning chef Scott Peacock cooks his

Bacon Fat, Beauty Aids & Fix-a-Flat

Having nothing to do with cooking, one Native American acquaintance, who insisted on anonymity, told me her mother used to use bacon fat to get the snarls out of her hair when she was a kid. It's not a new thing. Interestingly, the British Mrs. Beeton in her classic, mid-nineteenth-century tome titled *The Book of Household Management,* gives a recipe for pomade that calls for "half a pound of lard [make sure, she urges, that the lard be unsalted], two penny worth of castor oil and scent."

One step further towards trouble: the following recipe is from Jim Northrup, a Native American writer and newspaper columnist whose book *Rez Road Follies* is a favorite of mine.

"Q: What is Shinnob Viagra?

A: One part blueberry, one part moose meat, one part wild rice, one part commod pork, one part maple syrup, one part bacon grease, and 94 parts Fix-a-Flat."

To translate: "shinnob" is the Ojibway word for an Ojibwa Indian. "Commod" means "commodity." I had no clue what Fix-a-Flat was, so I looked it up. It's pretty much what it sounds like: spray-on stuff to seal the holes in flat tires. Amazing what bacon grease can do!

famous fried chicken in bacon fat. Food writer Francine Maroukian calls fat from really good bacon "a secret weapon in the kitchen. Just a few tablespoons will lend its smoky depth and salty twist to anything you cook." Gives me mental images of little bacon-tipped missiles fired out of under-counter silos toward stovetops all over the country. Which I guess would require Weight Watchers World Headquarters to respond with some sort of ABBM (Anti-Bacon Ballistic Missile).

5. *Big flavor return for a small investment*

As with olive oil, the flavor bacon brings to the table far exceeds its volumetric contribution. In other words, when you look at the ingredients for a recipe you'll rarely see either olive oil or bacon called for in particularly large quantity. But when you use them well, each makes an enormous difference in the flavor of the finished dish. Make the recipe for Meg Noori's macaroni with bacon fat, which you'll find at the end of this book, for example, and you'll see what I mean. Literally an ounce or so of bacon can make up half the flavor of a fantastic, easy-to-prepare dish.

In this sense I've become a bigger and bigger believer that bacon's biggest value in the kitchen isn't in its obvious uses, sliced for breakfast or BLTs (though those are great, too), but rather when it's chopped or diced and used as a seasoning. A bit of bacon goes a long way with long-cooked vegetables, just as olive oil does in Greek cuisine. Through slow-cooking the fat is absorbed into the produce, leaving a rich, full-flavored vegetable dish.

6. *Year-round cooking*

It's become much more commonplace in recent years to eat fresh foods when they're in season. But, while the flavor of both oil and bacon will vary a little from one time of the year to another (oil more so than bacon), both are really anything but seasonal. Each certainly has a season in which they were traditionally produced, but both were "designed" for relatively long storage and year-round use. And because both have long shelf lives they've become staples that cooks count on in all seasons, and in good economic times or bad.

7. Everyone eats it

Unlike some foods, which are eaten—or, were eaten at one time—only by particular social classes, both bacon and olive oil seem to be universally loved. While the wealthy may have had more of either, neither was ever produced only for rich people. Other than the obvious exception of observant Jews, Muslims and vegetarians, bacon is big with everyone—urban and rural, black and white, old and young. While they haven't added it as a question to the census yet, statistics indicate that over half of American households have bacon on hand at all times!

8. Different bacons for different dishes

Just as one would want to select an appropriate olive oil to use in a particular recipe (say, a big green oil with meat versus a soft elegant one for delicate fish), so, too, would I want to have more than one bacon on hand for cooking. Different dishes demand different levels of flavor intensity and smoke, and I want to be able to choose my bacon accordingly. In fact, this is one of my big pushes for the next few years: to get folks to move past thinking simply that they "like bacon," to realizing that pairing the right bacon with the right application makes for even better eating. In fact, the more you love bacon, the more you owe it to your bacon-loving self to explore the various flavors and contributions that different varieties can make to your cooking and eating pleasure.

9. Religion and politics

One place where I sort of struggled with testing the veracity of this "bacon as olive oil" theory was regarding the role that olive oil has in the spiritual history of the Mediterranean. Bacon just doesn't really play the kind of part in American religion that olives and olive oil do there. (Just as one example, "Christ" comes from the word "chrism," which means "to be anointed" in Greek, and the monarchs of Europe were anointed with olive oil.) But then I came

upon this quote from Joseph R. Conlin, who wrote about the Gold Rush-era West in *Bacon, Beans and Galantines*: "Then as now, most Americans probably preferred a good beefsteak on the table to any other viand. But pork was president of the Republic." It immediately struck me that I had been looking for the analogy in the wrong place. Politics is the true American religion. So whereas in Athens and Rome olive oil was connected to the gods, bacon in America took on the role of a duly-elected officer of state. As a writer in the nineteenth-century *Godey's Lady's Book* puts it: "The United States of America might properly be called the great Hog-eating Confederacy, or the Republic of Porkdom."

Maybe we should drop the bald eagle and replace it with a hog? Or maybe it's time to move past a "chicken in every pot" to "bacon in every skillet!"

10. The Tree Connection

There is actually a tenth way that olive oil and bacon are comparable. It's the tree connection. This was the toughest of the ten things on this list to work out. I mean, olives clearly grow on trees, but even city kids know that pigs don't. Or do they? One day I realized that there *was* a tree connection to be made! I've saved the story for the end of this book, but if you can't wait, skip ahead now—it's on page 134.

In the meantime . . . that's my theory. Take it if you like, leave it if you don't. Either way, eat your bacon!

Making Better Bacon

Like most traditional foods, bacon doesn't really leave you all that much to mess with. Either you do it right or you make the sort of stuff that accounts for 99 percent of what's sold in supermarkets. There are such huge quality differences—while the word "bacon" appears boldly on any number of pork products, you'll notice drastic differences from one brand to the next.

Nothing against nostalgia, but I've had little big-brand bacon that I would consider to be very good. When I was a kid, watching all those great Oscar Mayer commercials on TV, I really, really wanted to be able to eat their (non-kosher) products. I can still probably come up with the words to the jingle, and I was totally fascinated by Oscar Mayer Weiner whistles. (I actually have one at home. They debuted in 1952; the company gave one out gratis with every package of hot dogs. The song came later, hitting the airwaves in 1963.) Anyway, there are plenty of low-end brands of bacon just like Oscar Mayer, all selling for next to nothing and looking perfectly fine in the package. But while industrial product dominates the freezer cases of American supermarkets, it's pretty much everything you (or at least I) *don't* want in bacon. Pork from mass-produced, confinement-raised hogs that's been pumped with lots of water to keep the per-pound cost down: cook it up and it shrinks by a factor of about 50 percent when it hits a hot pan. In fact, the spatter and sizzle that so many folks have come to accept as the norm of bacon cooking is actually an indication that there's too much water in the meat. Not that you'd want to, but you could achieve much the same effect by buying better bacon and then dropping spoonfuls of water into the skillet while it cooks.

Mass-market bacon is also almost always loaded up with salt, primarily in an effort to mask the lack of flavor in an otherwise almost-tasteless meat. As a Spanish chef once told me about another famously salty food, in one of those not quite right but very endearing translations, "When you eat the bad anchovies, afterwards you can drink a fountain." It's the same story when it comes to mass-market bacon: if I eat a BLT in a greasy-spoon diner, hours later I'm still so thirsty I can barely cope. Inferior bacon also adds the lugubrious flavor of liquid smoke to the meat, trying to make up for the lost time and taste it would have gotten in a real smokehouse.

Happily, not all bacon is made for the mass market. There are still some great-tasting, full-flavored traditional offerings out there. So what makes them so much better?

The Raw Material: Breed and Feed

There's really no way around it—better bacon starts with better hogs. When George Orwell wrote in *Animal Farm* that "some animals are more equal than others," he wasn't referring to their culinary contributions, but he could have been. There's enormous variation in the flavor of the finished pork product depending on the breed of animal, where and how it's raised, and what it eats. In the same way that the flavor of free-range chickens sets commercial birds to shame, so too the standard commercial pork you and I are used to pales in comparison to some of the superb stuff being raised by true craftspeople.

This isn't some new thing—it's just going back to the way the best bacons were made a hundred years ago. In *Adventures of a Bacon Curer*, Maynard writes that, "Pig rearing in the eighteenth century was a very interesting business. All the landowners would vie with each other to breed the best pigs because that was the main source of meat to people who lived on the land." Traditional British breeds were rather bony and thin, and pigs were eventually brought over from China and Italy to cross-breed for a meatier hog. In his 1917 book *Bacon and Hams*, British author George J. Nicholls lists his six top breed choices as Lincolnshire Curly Whites, Berkshires, Tamworths, Large Blacks, Middle Whites and Large Whites. In each case he shares the breed's noteworthy characteristics. The Large White, he explained, had long sides, while the Yorkshire was considered best for Wiltshire bacon. Nicholls favored the Large Black: its high proportion of lean to fat made it "a good bacon pig."

Clearly it was understood that curers could pick their pig to suit the style of bacon they wanted to produce. Most of the artisan bacon-makers I'll be talking about in this book have been moving back to this idea. Many have taken up Berkshires as their breed of choice. Bruce Aidells, the culinary force (i.e., the flavor-maker of the finished meat, but not the farmer) behind Iowa's Vande Rose bacon, is equally adamant about Durocs—he thinks Berkshires have too much fat. Of course, not everyone agrees. Regardless of preference, though, what this means is that artisan curers are starting out with a big leg up on the commercial competition: their raw material is just so much more flavorful that the finished bacon is almost certain to taste better, too.

The hogs' diet also has an effect. George Nicholls makes clear that there are some things pigs should be kept away from: "Among the very worst foods," he wrote with great trepidation, "are turnips, mangolds and brewery or distillery grains." In his 1920 book, *Home Pork Making*, A. W. Fulton similarly advises against excessive feeding of corn, which is "rich in starch, is a great fat producer and should not be fed too freely in finishing off hogs for the best class of bacon."

On the positive side, Nicholls writes tantalizingly about pigs who were fattened in the peach fields at the end of summer. Citing studies by C. and T. Harris of Calne, in Wiltshire, he then concludes that, "the diets that give the best quality meat are, in order: barley and bran, barley and potatoes, barley and milk, barley and corn germs, and barley alone." Coincidentally, as I was writing this piece, I got a call from Nancy Newsom, Kentucky's cult superstar of country ham curing. "Have you ever had a hog who was raised on a barley diet?" she asked. Well, it's funny you should ask . . .

A lot of the lore about the history of Virginia country ham production centers on hogs that were fed peanuts. "Pigs are natural foragers," explained third-generation ham and bacon maker Sam Edwards, "and up until about the '50s, after the harvest the hogs were allowed to forage in the fields for the peanuts that didn't make the peanut wagon. But today they don't." Sam recently started putting peanuts back in his hogs' diet, and the early results are very promising.

I'm sure all this stuff is old hat to any quality-minded hog farmer or bacon maker. But it's interesting in terms of helping home shoppers get at better bacon. While it may seem inordinately technical, asking what type of pig was used or what kind of feed the animals were finished with really isn't any different than asking vendors at your local farmer's market what variety of tomato they're selling, or whether they used chemicals on their plants.

Another factor worth considering in evaluating good bacon is whether the hogs were allowed to move freely in the pasture. Ironically, traditional methods of production probably held on in American pig farming longer than they did in many other areas of agriculture that succumbed to mid-century industrialization in the quest for longer shelf life and lower cost. As recently as 40 years ago most hogs on Iowa farms were still running free. Unfortunately, the late 1970s and early '80s brought a push to get the pigs out of the pasture and into the same sort of confinement buildings that had become the norm for the nation's giant poultry producers. The quality of pork suffered as a result. "If you get a pig excited prior to slaughter," Maynard warns in *Secrets of a Bacon Curer* (his second bacon book), "the cure never takes, so it is very important that you know where they come from."

The shift to better sourcing has possibly moved more slowly in bacon making than it has with fresh pork. Makes sense, in that the improvement in flavor may be less immediately apparent after you've cured and smoked the meat. Most old-time bacon producers—like old-time cheesemakers—also feel the almost oppressive weight of mass-market pricing, and so have been reluctant to switch to a more costly raw material. Still, pretty much everyone seems to agree that the best-tasting pork—for bacon or any other use—comes from hogs that have been allowed to run free. The animals are living in a more natural habitat, they move around, they exercise, they get sun and fresh air. And they eat better when they're grazing (yes, hogs graze!) in the pastures. Niman Ranch has a very strict set of requirements for its producers—the sows nest in open little igloo-like buildings instead of the closed crates favored by confinement farmers, and antibiotics are never used. An ever-growing number of small family farms are following suit.

Sourcing is also about buying pork that's well-balanced for bacon making. Sam Edwards, who grew up in the ham and bacon business in Surry, Virginia, where his grandfather started curing in the early years of the twentieth century, said that it's critical to start with fresh belly that has the right lean-to-fat ratio: "We used to think leaner was better," he told me, "but the new lean generation of hogs has created the problem of bellies getting too lean." Bruce Aidells said much the same thing, stressing balance in all elements of bacon making—in this case, between fat and lean in the meat.

Note that while the old expression about "eating high on the hog" meant that the cuts from the upper part of the pig were the most prestigious and expensive, these days demand for bacon has made pork bellies ever more costly.

The Cure

The better old-style bacons are often dry-cured: rubbed with dry salt and sometimes sugar, nitrite or nitrate. Alternatively they can be wet-cured: soaked in a brine of saltwater and much the same stuff that goes into the dry cure. As with country ham, you had to have an environment in which the bacon would cure. Weather that was either too wet or too cold (freezing) could be a problem. Wet-curing has a long history: there are many recipes from the nineteenth century and even earlier that call for brining the raw belly to cure it before smoking. One of the key differences between the two styles is in yield: dry-cured varieties can lose up to 15, 20 or even 30 percent of their weight during curing, whereas commercial wet cures can actually gain weight while they're "working out." For a product that's sold by the pound, this often makes wet cures more attractive to the mass-market producers.

Wet or dry, the length of the cure can range anywhere from a day up to several weeks. Some producers use sea salt, others rely on commercial ground salt—there are actually dozens of different salts available and each producer of course swears by his or her own. And there are just as many choices for sugar. Most people stick with white, but some use brown. Maynard notes that darker, natural brown sugars like Demerara, Muscovado and even "black" sugar were used in Britain back in the old days. I've yet to find anyone doing that today, but it's only a matter of time before they start.

Phosphates are an ingredient that often signals the difference between cheap bacon and the really good stuff; industrial producers often add them to increase the meat's water content. Nor do the good guys use artificial flavors or colors.

On the other hand, although there has been much controversy around the use of nitrites or nitrates, even most of the artisan bacon makers do usually use one or the other. As a non-scientist, I had to struggle to get my head around this one. Both have been in use in some form or another for many thousands of years, but the modern-day concern arises from a series of articles in the 1980s that alleged that they were dangerous. At the time, some not-very-mindful producers were pumping large quantities of nitrites into their bacon. After finding that such noxious levels could indeed cause problems, the FDA eventually set a reasonable limit of 200 parts per million. Everything I've learned says that nitrates and nitrites aren't a threat in the quantities you and I consume in our bacon. Nitrites do help to stop bacon from turning gray, and also provide a basic level of food safety. The real question from a labeling standpoint is whether nitrite was added "inside" another ingredient or not. So, for instance, some natural supermarket chains have house brands of bacon that use spinach or celery juice in their cure. Others rely on sea salt. All of these substances have naturally occurring nitrates and nitrites, even if they're not listed as such. Happily you can find brands both with and without nitrites, so you can make your own decision and eat good bacon either way. Incidentally, brands that use vegetable juice are required by the FDA to call their bacon "uncured," which may be legally sound, but is also misleading, in that the bacon is still cured in either a wet brine or in dry salt (with or without sugar).

The Smoke

Although immersing oneself in, and absorbing significant amounts of, smoke is generally acknowledged to reduce human lifespan, it has very much the opposite effect on pork. In the old days, smoke was important not just to enhance the flavor of the bacon, but also because it helped reduce the risk of spoilage. These days all the bacon makers will tell you that smoke is about flavor, color and tradition. Although there are a few exceptions, most American bacons are smoked anywhere from a few hours to a few days. Different producers use different woods, and each wood of course brings its own flavor to the bacon. Maynard writes about throwing juniper berries, coriander and other spices in with the wood to alter the smoked flavor of his finished bacon.

Traditionally, the placement of the smokehouse was another important factor. As Maynard writes, "If you put [it] in the wrong place, too much in the wind, the sawdust burns very fast. Or if you put it in too sheltered a place, the sawdust smoulders and that is not right. You have to site the smoke in just the right area."

Similarly, A. W. Fulton wrote in *Home Pork Making* that, "Cloudy and damp days are best for smoking meat. It seems to receive the smoke more freely in such weather, and there is less danger of fire." (The latter I'd never have thought of but back in those days, fire was a daily risk for smokers. Even in more modern times, Morrilton Packing, maker of Arkansas peppered bacon, has twice had to rebuild after fires—once when the original shop went down back in

1928 and again when the entire plant burned in 1946.) Fulton goes on to say that, "The smoke need not be kept up constantly, unless one is in a hurry to sell the meat. Half a day at a time on several days a week, for two or three weeks, will give the bacon that bright gingerbread color that is generally preferred." By contrast, for those in more of a hurry, "The work of smoking may be finished up in a week, if one prefers, by keeping up the smoke all day and at night until bedtime."

In short, although meat-smoking equipment has become more scientific, most every bacon maker I've talked to says that their work is still essentially an art and a craft. As Harriette Arnow writes in *Seedtime on the Cumberland,* "smoking was an art of which there was no exact recipe; upriver many preferred a very low fire of green hickory chips, made of rather small limbs with the bark on. One did one thing and the next another; some after curing with smoke, and others before, dipped the meat in boiling water and then placed it in a shed to prevent insect trouble, but then it wouldn't get any nice mold. Whatever they did, was an old story by the time the Cumberland was settled; Virginia hams were already famous, and English history does not go behind English bacon."

The Sensory Buildup of Great Bacons

It seems funny to me that the modern world pays so much less attention to its choice of bacon than to the selection of other foods and drinks. Hardly anyone I know has a particular bacon that they swear by for a given recipe. People just seem to *like bacon.*

I want to push the envelope. If this book succeeds, it might get you to start taking notes on which bacon you want to use for a specific occasion: which bacon to wake up with and which one to have with heirloom tomatoes; which bacon goes best with your grits in the morning, which is best suited to eat with sweets, and which would be the best to take on a trip.

So how do you know a great bacon from a bad one? Regardless

Who's Uncle Sam?

Pork has been the key ration of every American army since the time of the Revolution. In fact, the initial "Uncle Sam" was a 21-year-old from New Hampshire by the name of Samuel Wilson. During the War of 1812 he was a prime pork packer for the Army. The story goes that he became quite popular among the troops for his provisioning work and upbeat personality. Barrels of pork labeled "U.S." came to stand for "Uncle Sam" Wilson, the man who fed the folks in the Army.

of how you're using it, when you eat good bacon the flavors should be in balance. You should taste each ingredient—pork, salt, smoke, sugar—without any one of them overwhelming the others. And you shouldn't be dying of thirst when you're done eating.

George Nicholls noted back in 1917 that the three keys are "the sense of touch, smell and taste." "Behind each," he explains, "there must be experience." It's interesting to me how these principles hold true nearly a hundred years later . . .

Texturally, good bacon should be neither too soft nor too hard. Oversoftness is usually a sign of undercuring or excess water, the latter leading to splattering and shrinkage. Extreme firmness, on the other hand, comes from too much salt, which will bear out in the flavor.

Then there's the smell. The romance of bacon has always been as much about its aroma as its flavor. Even bad bacon can smell pretty good in the pan. The same principle applies to coffee in the pot. In fact, the two together equal the classic smell of the breakfast-time American kitchen. Even bacon that is long out of the smoker should still smell good, with no hint of mold, the refrigerator or liquid smoke. Again, we're looking for complexity, balance and finish.

Speaking of smells, I'd often wondered what it was like to grow up living down the block from the Deli: every morning you'd wake up with the smell of Nueske's applewood-smoked bacon in the air. Then one day, while I was out running, I realized that I could just ask Tanya Nueske, since she grew up with that same great aroma. "There's still nothing like the smell of bacon in the house," she recalls. "It's a 'welcome home feeling' . . . like a campground fire. And when I went to school all the boys liked me :-), or at least they liked my 'perfume.'"

I chuckled at her answer, but didn't take it all that seriously until I came across an article in *The New Yorker* in which Tania Sanchez, co-author of *Perfumes: The Guide*, said that, "The question that women casually shopping for perfume ask more than any other is this: 'What scent drives men wild?' After years of intense research, we know the definitive answer. It is bacon." Which, I realize, leads us back to my Ojibwa friend's mother putting bacon grease in her hair.

Meet
the Bacons

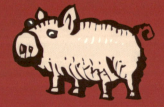

In keeping with my olive-oil analogy, I think the following bacons are the equivalents of the great estate-bottled olive oils. While so many olive oils come to us from the romantic Mediterranean—small hilltop villages, farms in the shadow of ancient Roman cities, centuries-old family estates—nearly all of the great American bacons are being made in the nation's backwoods. Unless you're really into bacon, Wittenberg, Wisconsin; Morrilton, Arkansas; Surry, Virginia; Madisonville, Tennessee; and Finchville, Bremen and Cadiz, Kentucky, sound more like the tour stops for a bluegrass band than entries in *Travel and Leisure*'s list of top destinations. But these are the places where the best bacon is made. Pretty much all the producers are hands-on folks who have stubbornly upheld a generations-long commitment to quality in the face of a persistent market push for low-cost product.

The list that follows certainly isn't meant to be some sort of perfect scientific study. It's just what I've tasted and liked over the years. So if your beloved bacon didn't make the book, by all means let me know about it at baconbits@zingermans.com.

I'd say try them all. Invite your friends over for a bacon tasting. Go wild. Hog-wild, even.

Wet-Cured Bacons

Nueske's Applewood-Smoked Bacon from Wisconsin

Take it from the late and very great R. W. Apple of the *New York Times:* Nueske's is "the beluga of bacon, the Rolls-Royce of rashers." Its flavor is meaty, subtly sweet (I think as much from the applewood as from the sugar in the cure), moderately smoky and so good that we've been cooking it every single morning at the Deli for over 27 years.

Tanya Nueske, granddaughter of the founder, Robert Nueske, is as passionate about her product as you can get. She's also a poster child for the benefits of a bacon-based existence: she's in her mid-thirties ("older than I look and younger than I feel"), lively, lovely, eats bacon all the time but stays in good shape. And even though she's been around applewood-smoked bacon her entire life, she still loves to talk about it, sell it and eat it. "I eat bacon so much," she told me. "I eat it plain all the time. We used to do some toasted buns with olives, sautéed onions, bacon and cheese and sour cream. You put them under the broiler— it's so good. We also take our hot dogs and we split them down the middle and add cheddar cheese and a pickle and wrap the whole thing in bacon and run it under the broiler." (You'll find a recipe for these "Wittenberg Splits" in the Recipes section). "Basically," she

added, stating the by-now obvious, "we use bacon with everything!"

If Tanya's bacon wasn't so darned good, her bubbliness could seem silly. Instead, it comes across as what it is—a sincere love for her product. "What we do is a very old tradition," she told me. "My grandfather started up selling the bacon in 1933. He started out smoking over applewood. And he had a way of doing it and a style that came from his grandparents." Robert's grandparents (Tanya's great-great-grandparents), Wilhelm and Wilhelmina Nueske, came to Wisconsin from Prussia in 1882, exactly 100 years before we opened the Deli.

Given what I've already said about the importance of raw materials, it's no surprise that bacon this good starts with special pork. Nueske's favors high-quality hogs, which they crossbreed with Pietrain pigs for the latter's excellent lean-to-fat ratio. The Pietrain is an old breed with shortish legs and a white hide with biggish black spots. They're named for the Belgian village in which the breed was apparently discovered centuries ago. "We work with a private supplier who raises their own hogs on family farms," Tanya says. "They transport, slaughter, process and ship via their own trucks. Also, they grow their own feed and use sustainable practices in farming while humanely raising the animals. What the hogs are fed plays a huge part in flavor and quality. We do a feed that's mostly a wheat and corn mixture. We've been working with our suppliers for well over 25 years. And we still hand-trim everything."

The Nueskes cure fresh slabs of bacon in brine for at least 24 hours, hang them to dry for a day or so, and then smoke them for at least another day. "When you smoke slowly over genuine applewood embers for a full 24 hours, the sweetness of the smoke really has a chance to permeate each cut of meat and impart our signature flavor," she says. They approach the smoking process as a craft. "We design our smokehouses ourselves and have them built for us," she explains. "The smoking is all hand controlled by the smokemaster but it's still a very artisan thing." She laughs, "The smokehouses are like children. The smokemaster will tell you that each smoke-

Slices of Plastic-Sealed Pork History

As Tanya Nueske's late-nineteenth-century ancestors were establishing themselves in the bacon business up in Wittenberg, a fellow German immigrant who had arrived in the States nine years before them was moving the same basic product in a totally different direction. Oscar Mayer founded the firm that still bears his name on the north side of Chicago in 1900. Although his brand is now about as commonplace as Kellogg's Corn Flakes, in his day Mayer was quite the industrial innovator. His firm was the first to sell pre-sliced and plastic-packaged bacon, back in 1924. Interestingly, the Oscar Mayer company was later sold to Kraft foods, founded and run in Chicago by J. L. Kraft, the man who sold the first pre-cut and plastic-sealed pieces of cheese. Not sure what it is about Chicago that leads everyone to want their food sliced and sealed in plastic, but there's clearly some kind of pattern here!

house is different." "And we still use actual applewood logs," she goes on. "People should know that 'applewood smoke' can mean almost anything these days—apple juice, apple smoke flavoring, liquid smoke . . . . But we only use real logs of Wisconsin applewood."

Over all these years Nueske's has remained one of the most popular foods we sell anywhere in our organization. Its flavor is on the mellower side: the soft sweetness from the applewood seems to amplify the natural sweetness in that high-quality pork the family goes to such lengths to source. We sell lots of Nueske's at the Deli, and lots more to folks who cook it in their own kitchens. If you visit you can try it on any number of Zingerman's sandwiches, in the greens at the Roadhouse or the Bacon Peppered Farm Bread from the Bakehouse. It's also become a big hit on what we call the 24-7 Burger: the bacon, smoked for 24 hours, laid across a couple of slices of seven-year-old Wisconsin cheddar, which in turn have been melted over a burger freshly ground from Niman Ranch beef.

Arkansas Peppered Bacon and Bacon with Long Pepper

One of my long-time favorites, this special pepper-coated bacon is cured and smoked in the foothills of the Ozarks. Like the Nueskes, the family's origins are in Germany: Felix Schlosser came over in 1922 and found Little Rock enough to his liking that he decided to stay in the area. He ended up opening a meat market in the small town of Morrilton, about 50 miles northwest of the state capital. His family is still using his recipes. Like Nueske's, they start with a wet cure—the trimmed bellies go into a brine of water seasoned with salt, sugar and spices (the exact proportions are still a family secret)

for four or five days. After a drying period that allows the smoke to penetrate properly (all good bacon makers do this) the slabs are smoked over hickory for just under 24 hours, then rolled in brown sugar and hand-rubbed with cracked black pepper.

Part of what I love about this bacon is that it's less sweet but still nicely spicy and very meaty—so meaty in fact that it's not my bacon of choice when I'm rendering fat or using the bacon as an ingredient in another dish. (I'd class that as a good problem, but if you're using it in recipes you might want to plan ahead by buying a bit more or having a little extra fat on hand.) It is darned good stuff, though. As Rick Strutz, one of our managing partners at the Deli, said while eating it on a pimento cheese sandwich, "Damn, I could eat this bacon all day!"

The peppered bacon is pretty much excellent on everything from burgers (especially with a well-aged cheddar, or the just-mentioned pimento cheese) to egg dishes. One really great way to use it is in the braised bacon recipe from Molly Stevens' award-winning book, *All about Braising*. Molly learned the dish while working with Judy Rodgers at Zuni Café in San Francisco. The recipe is far too involved to recount here, but basically it calls for a nice slow braise of a large chunk of bacon with vegetables in broth. What comes out of the pot then becomes the basis for an American version of pasta carbonara. The braising enriches the flavor of the bacon in a big way, and I really like the way the pepper livens up the carbonara.

While the folks in Morrilton have been making "regular" peppered bacon for sixty-odd years, their long pepper version is something new. I first read about long pepper while studying up on ancient Roman recipes and histories of the spice trade, but I didn't actually try it until I got some from Ben and Blair Ripple, who work with a series of small farms on the island of Bali. Like everything I've ever gotten from the Ripples, the long pepper was phenomenally flavorful. Each "pod" is composed of an inch or so long series of little black "peppercorns" that merge together into a cone as they grow. The flavor is definitely in the same family as black pepper, but with interesting high notes and a sweet, round fruitiness that's really lovely. Where Tellicherry black pepper's flavor is direct with nice winy undertones, the Balinese long pepper is more of a roller coaster ride of exotic flavors that play out in twists and turns on the palate. It makes for some very interesting, very sensual, very spicy eating.

In its heyday, long pepper was actually more popular with Roman cooks than black pepper, and sold for about three times the price (and remember, back then a pound of black pepper sometimes commanded a higher price than gold). It passed out of use in Europe during the Middle Ages, most likely because it's moister than black pepper and hence didn't offer the latter's keeping qualities. I was surprised to find that long pepper showed up in recipes for sauces, vinegars and pickles in Colonial-era cookbooks, but its use in that context drove our desire to create this very tasty cured pork belly.

You can, of course, use the long pepper bacon with sandwiches and eggs. But because of its more interesting, complex finish, I really like it with sweet ingredients: it's nice with citrus, or sprinkled over an autumn salad of apples, toasted nuts and very good lettuces. It's also great chopped and liberally sprinkled over a warm poached egg atop a salad of fresh frisée. To add an extra dimension, you can also try any of these same dishes topped with a bit of orange-olive oil (i.e., an oil for which the olives and oranges have been pressed together, not a lower-end version where orange oil has been added after the pressing has already taken place).

Dry-Cured Bacons

Edwards' Bacon from Virginia

The story of Edwards' country ham and bacon is so storybook it seems too good to be true, but true it is, so why not tell it? The Edwards family has been curing pork products in Surry, Virginia, for over a hundred years, and best I can tell they've been doing it darned well for pretty much that whole time. If a sense of history matters to making high-quality, true-to-its-roots food, then the Edwards have a big advantage. Some of the very first hogs in the colonies landed at Hog Island, just across the river from Surry, in the early seventeenth century. The island's watery boundaries made it easy to keep the hogs from wandering away.

The family's history with pork began in 1925, when Sam Edwards' grandfather started serving passengers his homemade ham sandwiches while captaining the ferryboat his father had started on the cross-river route between Surry and Jamestown

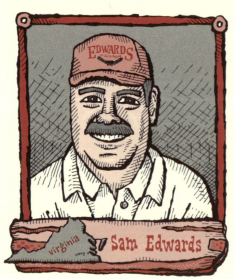

Island. True to the history of Hog Island, the boat was named after Captain John Smith, who first claimed the island for the British Crown. Interestingly, the Edwards family recently found the wheelhouse from that original ferryboat down at the end of a private pier on the Elizabeth River, a tributary of the James River about 45 minutes upstream from Surry. It was no small thing to get the boat back home, but the historically minded Edwards felt it was worth the trouble. "We had to float it off the pier, cut it in half and truck it in from a Norfolk marina," Sam recalls. The ham that Sam's grandfather served on that ferry was cured just as he'd learned to do on the family farm. He gained such acclaim for his sandwiches that in 1926 he started a business to sell whole hams. Bacon and sausage followed soon after.

With all that background it's no shock I suppose that Sam Edwards still makes some seriously good bacon and ham eighty-plus years down the road (or maybe I should say, "down the river"?). The curing and smoking is still done pretty much the way his grandfather and father did it in their time. (Actually, Sam's dad still stops in a couple of times a week to make sure Sam hasn't strayed from the porky path.) "I've been making bacon, ham, and sausage since I was 13 and full-time since the late Seventies," he told me. While it's a subject for another essay, I'm also a big fan of their traditional (labeled as "Wigwam") country hams and their sage-seasoned breakfast sausage. But since today's topic is bacon I'll stick to cured pork belly.

Like most of the producers I discuss in this book, Sam Edwards is making country-cured bacon the way it has been done for centuries. "We start with fresh pork belly that has the right lean-to-fat ratio," Sam told me. "Ninety-nine percent of bacon today, water is the first ingredient. But we dry cure. We literally rub it with salt and sugar. We leave the bacon in the salt and sugar for seven to 10 days. Then we rub it off and smoke the bellies for about 18 to 24 hours over green hickory to get the color and flavor we want." The best bacons aren't ready the moment they're taken out of the smoker. "Part of the process that folks forget about is to let it hang for at least a week or so afterwards, to let it temper up right," Sam said. "It loses a little more moisture and takes on a better flavor, I think."

Having dealt with a lot of multi-generational family food businesses over the years, I wouldn't have been at all shocked to find that someone in Sam's third-generation position was passively disinterested in the family business, or that he was abandoning time-honored tradition for business school "solutions" like rapid sales growth in the middle of the cured meat market. Or, alternatively, that he was rigidly unwilling to alter anything at all, for fear of losing a longstanding clientele. Happily, Sam seems to have achieved the same sort of balance in his business approach that cooks enjoy in his bacon. He is continually experimenting and innovating in the interest of producing ever-better pork, but always while staying true to the Surry roots of his grandfather's and his father's work. Sam still dry-cures all of his bacon, for example. But he also recently started reintroducing the old tradition of peanut-finishing his hogs. He has also started buying pork from old breeds like the Berkshire. Most recently, he has started testing pork from pigs that have been finished on plums at the end of the season. By the time you read this, it's safe to say he'll have tested ten other things too, knowing that they won't all work but that one or two small innovations (or more often "restorations") will help make for better-tasting bacon.

The flavor of Edwards' bacon is sweet and smoky at the same time, terrific for eating as is on sandwiches, or for flavoring anything from Hoppin' John to cornbread to seafood stew. For reasons that I can't really explain this is also the bacon I like best with eggs. It's definitely a bacon for bigger-flavored dishes. Although Sam prefers it cooked on the soft side, I prefer it more crisply cooked myself. It's darned good chopped and tossed on a big bowl of grits (the good ones, like Anson Mills: I have exceedingly low patience for low-level industrial grits), along with eggs over easy and a couple of slices of top-notch toast. And speaking of toast, Edwards' is equally great on a toasted fried-egg sandwich.

The bottom line on the subject from the man himself? "In my opinion, true dry-cured bacon, made with the simplest ingredients, makes the best end product . . . and of course hickory smoked."

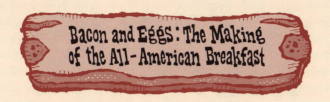

Bacon and Eggs: The Making of the All-American Breakfast

A century ago, most urban Americans were pretty happy just grabbing a couple of slices of toast and coffee for breakfast. But a man by the name of Edward Bernays changed all that. As a public-relations pioneer, Bernays has been called both "the father of spin" and "the most influential man you've never heard of." In his theory of PR, which he called "the engineering of consent," he argued that, "If we understand the mechanism and motives of the group mind, it is now possible to control and regiment the masses according to our will without their knowing it."

In the mid-1930s Bernays was working for Beechnut. While the company had long sold bacon, its sales were down and Bernays was struggling to find a way to get them back up. So he used his uncle Sigmund Freud's (you read that right) psychological approaches to help convince the public that, among other things, bacon and eggs was the true all-American breakfast. He set up a national medical survey which "proved" that eating a hearty breakfast was the healthy way to go. He then sent the report out to five thousand physicians around the country, accompanied by a packet that talked about the value of eating bacon and eggs each morning. Seems to have worked darned well, since it's hard to imagine a more typical start to the American day than a couple of strips of bacon with eggs, toast and a steaming cup of coffee.

If you prefer cereal with bananas to bacon for breakfast, you might find it interesting that Bernays later went on to lead the "marketing" of the U.S. government/United Fruit Company-sponsored coup in Guatemala in 1954.

Unsmoked Kentucky Bacon from Finchville Farms

Half an hour east of Louisville, Bill Robertson makes a very good, dry-cured but unsmoked country-style bacon. "You don't smoke at all?" I asked, surprised to find someone selling a Southern bacon that hasn't been in close proximity to smoldering wood. "Just Lucky Strikes," he answered, "I still smoke those."

"What we do isn't fancy," Bill went on, "but it's traditional for this region." I certainly haven't found any other place in America that's doing anything similar. His bacon is cured for ten to fourteen days in salt, sugar, red and black pepper. They don't add any nitrite or nitrate. "We use a brown sugar," Bill related. "And I don't know why. I guess we do it because my dad did it." After the cure, the slabs are allowed to air dry for another two to three weeks, enhancing and concentrating the flavors. The curing process leaves the slabs weighing about 18 percent less than they did when they came into the plant.

"Our bacon isn't a regular bacon. It's a green bean seasoning product," he told me with great seriousness. "People in this region have been using country bacon—dry-cured and air-dried like this—for years. Green beans are pretty bland. But you get the bacon in

there . . ." Even over the phone I could tell that he was smiling at the fond memories.

Intrigued, I went to the Finchville website the next day to order some of the stuff, but the bacon was nowhere to be found. I called Bill back and asked him if I'd missed it. "No," he said, "we took it off of there because we had so many complaints about it being too salty." I told him

I'd be glad to order some. "I'll send you some to try," he volunteered. "But remember, it's *not* a bacon for slicing. You can pan fry it but it's pretty strong. It's a seasoning bacon." I think he warned me about this four times in the space of 15 minutes. After I promised at least four times in return not to serve it with my morning eggs he agreed to send me a sample.

The bacon arrived in Ann Arbor five days later, a chunk of cured, never-seen-smoke pork belly about four inches by two inches and an inch-and-a-half thick. Troublemaker and anarchist that I am, I really wanted to slice it up and serve it to someone with eggs, just to see what would happen. But I'd promised, so I stuck to Bill's instructions and cooked it with green beans. Sure enough, when used the way he'd described, the results were outstanding.

In studying the region of Kentucky and Tennessee from whence Bill Robertson hails, I discovered that his description of his bacon as a "bacon for green beans" was no arbitrary choice. In *Seedtime on the Cumberland*, Harriette Arnow includes the following great description of the dish as it was prepared at the end of the eighteenth century, and still during her own childhood more than a century later:

"Beans for next day were picked late in the afternoon into a basket or a tucked-up apron, and when the early supper was finished, the woman, often a grandmother, if she could see well sat with them in her apron, broke off the ends, pulled off the strings, and broke them into pieces. Next morning they were put into a kettle, iron of course, and cooked during breakfast getting; after breakfast they were taken to the springhouse and changed and washed through two or three waters. They were put on the fire again, outside in hot weather, and this time a large chunk of cured hog meat, jowl bacon would do in beans, sliced down to the skin, but with the water-scrubbed skin left on was put in. Beans and bacon cooked along until noon; you could eat a few for dinner, but they were better left simmering along till supper."

Sometimes, the true skill in leadership is the ability to quietly make those around you look better. I think Bill's bacon does something similar taste-wise. I've used it as a seasoning with squash, greens, fish and half a dozen other things, and just as Bill said it has added a whole mess of flavor to whatever else went into the pot. And, of course, it's great with those fresh green beans. You just have to promise not to eat it sliced with eggs, okay?

Benton's Bacon from Eastern Tennessee

I've been refraining from my usual habit of peppering my essays with lists, but now I'll succumb and give you:

Three Really Big Reasons to Try Benton's Bacon

1. This is Southern Foodways Alliance leader, food writer and exceptionally tasteful individual of great character and outstanding word selection John T. Edge's favorite bacon.

2. Allan Benton is, seriously, one of the nicest people I've ever met, in the food world or out.

3. Benton's bacon is really good—very special stuff with big, impossible-to-miss flavor.

John T. isn't the only one who believes—Benton's bacon has been written up in the *New York Times, Gourmet, Saveur* and probably just about every other major food magazine. It's a favorite of acclaimed Momofuko chef David Chang. I could go on listing the famous fans, but I won't: suffice to say it's a long and prestigious list. Of course, for me, it's really about how the stuff tastes, not about some signup sheet of celebrity endorsements. So when I finally got down to Benton's recently, I had the chance to ask Allan the obvious question: "What makes the stuff so great?" He smiled, looked me in the eye, and finally, in the slow, soft always-upbeat way that I've come to love about him, he said, "Well, Ari, the secret is that there is no secret. This is just the way bacon was made years ago."

The production methods that Allan learned growing up are similar to what Sam Edwards and others are doing, but with his family's own western Virginia mountain twist. For starters, Allan's gradually moving most of his production to Berkshire pork, and I'd guess within a few more years Benton's bacon will be produced only from the bellies of heirloom breeds. The freshly arrived bellies get a rubdown with brown sugar and salt. After a couple weeks of curing they're rinsed and re-rubbed with more salt and sugar, then

left to cure for another two weeks. Finally the bacon gets about 48 hours in the smoker, mostly over hickory.

The length of the cure and the long smoke time (nearly twice what most folks do) are clearly the biggest contributors to the intensity of the Benton's flavor. This is not a bacon that lingers casually out on the edge of your eating. It's a deep confluence of smoke, salt and sweet: none dominates, all are pronounced. It's like umami all in one bacon bit. I know plenty of good cooks who find it too much for their taste. But in the same way that people who love a great glass of stout or porter have a hard time with lighter beers, so, too, are Benton's fans reluctant to leave their longtime favorite off the menu.

If you get on a Benton's BLT roll, you can try it with a cornmeal-coated fried catfish filet or some fried green tomatoes. But my favorite thing is to serve it—and its fat, in all its smoky glory—over a bowl of hot mush made from exceptional Anson Mills cornmeal. While it probably sounds plain, that simple dish, made with two incredibly good ingredients, is actually amazingly delicious. I think of it as the Southern equivalent of eating just-cooked Martelli spaghetti tossed in a great Tuscan olive oil and topped with freshly grated Parmigiano-Reggiano and black pepper.

Father's Bacon from Central Kentucky

On the outskirts of the tiny town of Bremen, about two hours south-west of Louisville, the Gatton family has been curing and smoking hams on the same farm since the 1840s. Charlie Gatton Jr., whom I met a few years back, has been curing pork since 1962. (It was his father, Charles Sr., who got the actual "business" going back in the mid-twentieth century.) Short and stocky, maybe in his late fifties, Charlie Jr., speaks with the same kind of Southern authenticity as Sam Edwards—it only takes about 10 seconds to understand that these guys grew up right where they're still at. Both geographically and emotionally, they and their bacons are well-rooted in the local terrain.

Charlie's passion for his bacon is huge, and he's not afraid to share it. Whether he's working a stand at a farmer's market, ship-ping it out through his mail-order catalog, or expounding its virtues pretty much anywhere else that he can get people to listen, Charlie loves selling his stuff. All I had to do was ask one question and he launched into a clearly oft-recited but heartfelt spiel: "If you read the label on most bacons," he fired off, "it's going to say water

first. Ours says 'salt, sugar, sodium nitrate.' But there's no water." He apparently moves loads of the stuff on QVC, where he likes to cook up a strip of supermar-ket bacon next to a strip of Father's just to show viewers the enormous difference in shrinkage.

In keeping with Char-lie's family recipe, Father's bacon slabs start out in a dry cure of salt, brown and white sugars, a bit of nitrite and some "secret ingredients." (Charlie utters this last phrase as if it had a meaning all its own, something you could order from your local food service supplier.) "It's a lost art to do bacon this way," he told me. "The bacon is in the salt and sugar for about 10 days or so, and it loses at least 12 percent during the curing. Nobody but me mixes the cure," he went on. "I even build the fires. The bacon is smoked over green hickory sawdust for two or three or four days." It's a serious country bacon eater's bacon. In terms of endorsement, it's probably worth knowing that this is the one that Nancy Newsom, of country ham acclaim, has chosen to sell from her store further west in Princeton.

Father's bacon business has grown enormously in recent years, from about 4,000 pounds a year up to 100,000. They're now making a plethora of flavored bacons in addition to the straight stuff the family started with. It's not really my thing, but if you're into it you can try his cinnamon-, chocolate- or vanilla-seasoned bacons. Personally, I go for their straight stuff, or at most the pepper-cured. Both the original and peppered varieties are intensely very smoky, perhaps the smokiest in this book. It's not subtle stuff, but sometimes that can be a good thing. Just an inch or two chopped up into a dish adds powerful pungency.

"The biggest thing," Charlie told me, "is you got to educate the people on the difference. Old fashioned, hand-done, genuine bacon . . . At the W Store [I assumed he meant Wal-Mart] you can get bacon for $2.59 a pound, but I guarantee it takes twice as much of theirs as ours."

Broadbent's Bacon from Southwestern Kentucky

When I first met Ronny and Beth Drennan they were still curing their hams and bacon in the town of Cadiz (although it's spelled the same way as the town in southern Spain, Kentuckians pronounce it like "Katy's") down in the southwestern corner of the Bluegrass

State. In 2008 they moved into a new plant about 25 miles up the road in Kuttawa. A particularly friendly person in a state that's known for its hospitality, Ronny is a real gentleman, soft-spoken with blue eyes, hair combed over his forehead, a little shorter than average but with big, meaty Popeye arms. His accent is intense, even by Kentucky standards, and he rubs his hands a lot while we talk: probably a blessing after all the time he has spent rubbing cure into pork. His equally friendly wife, Beth, was in the back room when I visited, boning and slicing country ham into packages. These folks clearly work hard, and it's not very glamorous work at that.

The Broadbent company and its cure recipe date back to 1909, when Anna and Smith Broadbent started selling smoked country ham, bacon and sausage from their farm. (Unique to Trigg County, the sausage is stuffed into cloth sacks. It's very good, but that's another story.) Smith Broadbent III, still lives on his family's farm at the end of Broadbent Road, behind the business. This is also where the ham house is located. Ronny and Beth bought it from Smith back in 1999, and Smith worked with them for a few years to transfer his family's knowledge and recipes.

This wasn't one of those "city kids falls in love with the country

and move to Cadiz to cure bacon" stories—Ronny and Beth are both from the area. "I grew up in a small town, on a dairy farm," Ronny told me. "My dad had 163 acres. Put six kids in college . . . four of them finished, but I'm not one of them. We had cattle, hogs, tobacco, a little bit of everything. We killed our own hogs, but we never really got to eat the ham that was made from them." Why not? Because the meat had become an important source of the family's income. Which reminded me how, by the middle of the nineteenth century, the separation of hog raising from hog eating had launched a downward spiral in quality, all in the name of modern efficiency.

What the Drennans are doing at Broadbent's is probably anything but efficient by industrial standards. "We hand-rub each belly with salt, sugar and a bit of nitrite," Ronny explained. "Then we stack them on the shelves about seven or eight slabs high. We leave them for one week, then we wash all the salt off and hang them up on the bacon hooks and we let them sit overnight and a day to set, then let them sit. Then we smoke them for three or four days. A lot of it depends on the weather—sometimes it'll smoke quicker and sometimes a bit longer."

Broadbent's bacon pushed me to the realization that long, dry-cured bacons (Edwards', Father's and Benton's are other examples) are akin to the big red wines at the end of a great wine list, or a seven-year-old cheddar in a cheese selection: they're not for everyone, and if you were only going to pick one item to sell this wouldn't be it. I used Broadbent's for a class I taught at the International Association of Culinary Professionals down in Dallas a few years ago, though, and it was the surprise hit of the session. Interestingly the people who were most excited about it were the food professionals: writers and chefs like Bruce Aidells and Molly Stevens who are interested in big flavors and hadn't tasted anything like it.

Broadbent's is great for stews or dishes where you want serious flavor. Of course, if you like country bacon (as I do) it's also very good with eggs and grits. That big taste might scare a few city folks, but it must taste like a bit of nostalgia if you grew up in the region. (Kentucky food guy Bob Perry is a self-described addict.) "Our bacon tends to remind people so much of what their grandparents did," Ronny told me. "They've moved off the farm and they get to taste this now. So many people say now that they remember their grandparents' bacon, but that they haven't had bacon like this in years."

A Few Other Good Bacons to Be Aware of

We don't carry the six bacons described in the following pages at Zingerman's right now, but they're very good and you'll definitely want to know about them.

Niman Ranch Bacon from Iowa

All the good things that go into making Niman's fresh pork so special also contribute to the quality of their bacon. Thanks to Paul Willis' strong views on proper hog raising, the process starts with very good fresh bellies. The hogs are all from the older, higher-fat, higher-flavor breeds like Farmer's Cross, Berkshire and Duroc. They run free in the pastures, are given no antibiotics and are slaughtered according to the strict protocols of New York's Animal Welfare Society. Niman's currently offers bacon in both wet-cured and dry-cured forms. Most of it is smoked over applewood, but they do some over maple, as well. Niman's also has a natural "uncured" applewood-smoked bacon, made with vegetable extract instead of nitrite or nitrate. All three varieties are quite tasty and pretty widely available in specialty supermarkets across the country, making Niman Ranch a good option for those who don't have access to some of the harder-to-find bacons in this book.

THORNTON, IOWA

Summerfield Farms Bacon from Virginia

Jamie Nicoll has been curing bacon at Summerfield Farms in Culpepper, Virginia, since the mid-1990s. Probably the richest of all the bacons on my list, Summerfield's is delicately smoked, sweet in a noticeable but not out-of-balance way and very delicious. Their simple process involves dry-curing fresh natural pork sides in brown sugar, molasses and kosher salt (with no nitrites). After the cure they're lightly smoked to 165°F over a six-hour period.

CULPEPPER, VIRGINIA

Because of Summerfield's high sugar and molasses content you might not cook it as long or at as high a heat as you would other bacons. Instead, you want to hold on to as much of the flavorful fat as possible. "If you don't burn it, that fat is so wonderful to cook other things with," Jamie said. "We also recommend that people cut it thicker to retain moisture. We've found that some folks aren't cooking it in the traditional way at all, but instead are boiling it so that you have a soft-cooked bacon without the caramelization. They seem to like it that way."

Burgers' Country Bacon from Missouri

Burgers' is one of the nation's biggest country ham producers, which isn't really all that big by commercial meat manufacturing standards. Steven Burger is the third generation in the business and has dedicated himself to preserving tradition while simultaneously improving most everything the company cures. From what people say, that's pretty much the way it has gone ever since Steven's grandfather, E. M. Burger, started the business in the 1950s. Burgers' recipes and curing routines may actually date back to the 1920s and the work his great-grandparents did on the family farm. The volume back then would have been similar to that of many entrepreneurial farmers, who were moving from curing just a ham or two for the family up to doing an extra half-dozen or so for sale to outsiders.

Within their modern, large-scale production facility the Burgers have retained a number of old-time traditions that are well worth experiencing. One of their most popular products is a mild and somewhat sweet, brine-cured "city bacon." My taste, though, runs to the fuller flavor of their old-style country bacon, which is dry-cured for seven to 10 days with salt, brown sugar and black pepper and  then smoked over hickory wood for about 12 hours. The long, dry cure gives it an intense pork flavor, but the fairly short smoking time keeps it from being as smoky as most of the other bacons here.

The Burgers also sell smoked pig jowl—the same cut that Italians would call guanciale (the word is pronounced as if a Boston native were saying "Go on, Charley": *G'won chaalie!*), although in this case it's not just cured but also smoked. While I'm sure the word "jowl" is likely to put off more than a few readers, it's actually one of the most flavorful parts of the pig. As Bill Lamb, one of the mountain folk interviewed in *The Foxfire Book*, says, "Now you talkin' about part of a hog that I love is th' jowls. They ain't a better tastin' bite'a meat in a hog than th' jowl." Down Missouri way, it seems they pronounce it both "jowl" as in "owl" and "joel" as in Billy, so you can ask for it either way.

You can use the jowl in your cooking just as you would bacon. Steven Burger recounts that a more traditionally Southern approach is to dice it up as seasoning for black-eyed peas. The Burgers also use it in a cornbread, black-eyed pea and smoked jowl stuffing. Or you could make a Missouri version of *pasta all'amatriciana*. Regardless, the Burgers' hog jowl is really quite delicious. Silky-smooth texture on the tongue and a whole lot of flavor from each strip.

Nodine's Bacon from Connecticut

One of the long-time premier bacon makers on the East Coast, Nodine's has been curing in Goshen, Connecticut, since 1969. They do a whole array of smoked meats (I'm a big fan of their smoked chicken breast), including a range of different bacons, all of which start with a wet cure of water, salt, sugar and nitrite. Two of these are particularly interesting to me. One is called apple-smoked. This doesn't mean apple *wood* smoked, as it does with Nueske's. Instead, in a tradition true to Nodine's New England roots, they smoke the bellies over apple pomace (the solids that are left over after fresh apples are pressed) from a local cider mill. "We dry it out after they deliver it, and put it in with some hardwood sawdust," says Ron Nodine, who founded the smokehouse 40 years ago. "We only smoke the pork about 12 hours. How long it's in there depends on which 'house' it's in. We don't want a real heavy smoke on it."

Indeed, the flavor is sort of sweet, lightly smoky—ideal, to state the obvious, for those who like their bacon on the lighter end of the spectrum. It's particularly nice with seafood.

Another tasty Nodine's offering is their juniper bacon, smoked over hardwood sawdust liberally spiced with dried juniper berries. Adding juniper to the mix isn't a new idea—Maynard mentions it as an old English technique in his *Adventures of a Bacon Curer*. Anyway, Nodine's juniper bacon has a bigger flavor than the apple-smoked version, though it's still relatively light on the smokiness scale.

Vande Rose Bacon from Iowa

This is a bacon that originates with Bruce Aidells, a nice Jewish boy who earned his Ph.D. in endocrinology and then got into food in a big way, first as a chef in the Bay Area and then by designing the line of fine sausages that still bears his name. Bruce has written a number of books in which, untrue to his Jewish roots, pork plays a leading role. I've come to think of him as the Burl Ives of bacon: both are big guys with big opinions, beards and a way with words—smart, creative types who aren't afraid to share their views on bacon (in Bruce's case, anyway; I don't know about Burl) or really anything else.

I'm not equipped to assess Bruce's expertise in endocrinology, but I can say that he's a talented writer, food scientist, chef and storyteller. Lately he's gotten himself hooked up with a trio of Dutch-descended families who are raising about 1400 heirloom hogs near Oskaloosa, Iowa. About 45 minutes southeast of Des Moines, the town was originally settled by Quakers back in the middle of the nineteenth century. The three Vande Rose families (*Van* Gilst, *De* Bruin and *Roze*nboom—get it?) arrived in the area in the 1850s. Their Quakerism and the natural beauty of their surroundings are fitting for the approach these three families have taken to hog-rearing: their animals are raised in a peaceful setting, roaming free in the pastures.

Looking to develop new products that they could sell alongside their already-acclaimed fresh pork, the families hired Bruce to do the culinary development work on a new line of bacons and hams. Everyone involved shared a strong belief in Duroc hogs: the three families have been raising the breed pretty much since they started farming in Iowa, 175 or so years ago, and Bruce feels that Durocs have a better lean-to-fat ratio than the Berkshires that other producers are so enamored of.

The Vande Rose bacon is a country cure. It's done dry, not with brine. "From my way of thinking you can't really beat that old way, what they call the 'box cure,' or the 'dry cure,'" Bruce said. But like Burgers' it's on the gentler side of the smoke spectrum. "A lot of bacons I think are too smoky," he said. "Really good bacon is all about balance. Salt, sugar and smoke. They should all be in balance. And the fat-to-lean too: the Duroc is really good for that." He's clearly pretty darned happy with the Vande Rose product. And it is, indeed, quite good.

Bruce likes to cook with his bacon, not just eat it straight up. "I make goulash with it," he says. "I start with bacon and then render out the fat. I like a little bit of bacon flavor but I don't want it be too smoky so this bacon is perfect for me." His wife, Nancy Oakes, who's long been doing amazing things with all sorts of food—including bacon—at her deservedly acclaimed Bay Area restaurant, Boulevard, uses bacon to wrap pork tenderloins and game birds. "She did these great Cornish hens with cornbread stuffing and then roasted them with bacon," Bruce recalled, reminiscing lovingly about both his wife and the aroma of the birds as she took them out of the oven (at least, I think he was talking about both . . .). Just as he said, the Vande Rose bacon is very good for cooking (and eating, too, of course). The mellower nature of the smoke enables it to accent a dish without overwhelming the other flavors.

Dreymiller and Kray Bacon from Illinois

If you're driving through northern Illinois you might want to watch for the bacon smoked and sold by Dreymiller and Kray. They do their curing and smoking in the out-of-the-way town of Hampshire. The firm evolved out of two separate businesses that were founded in 1929 by the Dreymiller brothers, who, like the Nueskes and Schlossers, had come over from Germany. Various in-and-out-of-the-family sales of the shop and smokery eventually delivered things into the hands of Floyd Reiser, who in turn passed them on to his son, Ed. Ed's pretty passionate about what he's doing. The bacon begins with a wet cure, and is then smoked over applewood logs that Ed goes out and cuts himself. Because his smokehouse isn't federally inspected, Ed's bacon can't be shipped over state lines, so you can only get it at specialty shops in Illinois. But it's worth a detour if you find yourself nearby.

HAMPSHIRE,
ILLINOIS

The Beautiful Sound of Bacon

In an interview on the media website *Pitchfork,* Tom Waits remarked that his favorite sound is bacon frying in a pan. "If you record the sound of bacon in a frying pan and play it back it sounds like the pops and cracks on an old 33 ⅓ recording," he said. "Almost exactly like that. You could substitute it for that sound."

And Waits certainly isn't alone in his love for the sound. Patrick Kavanagh, writing in *The Green Fool,* quipped that, "an empty stomach is a great egoist, and a bad listener to anything save the fizz of rashers on a pan."

Behind the Smokehouse Door:
A Visit to Benton's Country Bacon

While eating bacon is a great thing to do, there's something to be said for actually seeing, smelling and scoping it in its natural setting; no matter how much homework I might do, there's still really no all out, one-hundred-percent substitute for seeing it all *in situ*. Which is why, as much as I can (while doing everything else that I do), I try to get out to visit the folks who make the food we work with.

These firsthand visits to artisan producers are the part of my work that falls into the "I wish I had *your* job" category. People who hear me talk about my taste travels say something like that almost without fail. Hey, I do love my job. But you don't need an advanced degree to get on a plane and fly to some second-tier airport, arrange a rental car and drive out into the middle of nowhere to look at pork bellies sitting in salt or hanging in a smoker. You just have to be a little . . . shall we say, fixated on food. Of course, if you've read this far into the book without throwing it against the wall, then it's a pretty safe bet that you and I share this passion. So I suggest that you go on down and visit. As long as you're courteous and call ahead to let them know you're coming (tell them I sent you!), you're likely to be received with open arms. Have fun. Talk to the folks. See the sights. Smell the smoke. Help their sales and bring home some bacon.

Before you head for the airport, keep in mind that sometimes what you'll learn when you get there will be very different from what you thought you were going to find before you embarked on your journey. Which is exactly what happened when I took the trip down Route 411 to the eastern Tennessee town of Madisonville, where Allan Benton has been making great bacon for nigh on 40 years now. While it's no Route 66, 411 is memorable for its name if nothing else. I keep thinking of it as "four-one-one," as in "calling information," since my trip there was all about research. But folks down that way mostly seem to call it "four-eleven" (or more accurately "four-'leven"). Depending on how you look at things, the highway starts down in Leeds, Alabama, and runs almost exclusively through out-of-the-way rural areas. It ends not far from Madisonville (where Benton's is made), which coincidentally enough sits right near the base of the Great Smoky (get it?) Mountains.

I'd wanted to visit Benton's ever since John T. Edge started extolling its virtues to me nine or 10 years ago. Although it took me nearly a decade to actually get there, please don't assume that this is any reflection on the quality of the bacon. It's just that the route to Madisonville is pretty much a road less traveled: unless you need to go to Knoxville (which I never had); like to spend time camping in the mountains (I don't); or make regular trips to Pigeon Forge to experience Dollywood (not high on my life list), Madisonville's just not really on the way to anywhere most folks are likely to visit. Happily, in the fall of 2007 I was asked to speak at a Southern Foodways Alliance event at Blackberry Farms, a very fine luxury resort about 40 minutes from Madisonville. So after quickly dropping my bags off at Blackberry on a sunny January day, I rounded up a few fellow bacon-lovers and finally, eagerly made my way to Benton's to taste this very smoky bacon at its source.

If you hadn't read this before going, your first reaction to Benton's would probably be pretty similar to mine. I was immediately struck by how unprepossessing the place was. Like Allan Benton himself, the smokehouse is anything but fancy. In fact, it's about as down-home as you're going to get. I suppose it's possible that a few interior designers have stopped in to purchase pork over the years, but I also feel pretty safe in speculating that none of them stuck around to help out with the décor. I offer this commentary only so that you don't have the kind of reaction we sometimes see at the Deli in first-time customers who have been hearing about Zingerman's for years: they walk into the place, scrunch up their foreheads, squinch their eyes, and say, "That's it? It's so *small*..." While Benton's is now much-talked-about and highly praised, you need to understand that this isn't a million-dollar pork palace; if you need a big production, head back down to Dollywood.

Allan Benton bought the building that now houses Benton's Smokehouse back in 1978, and I don't think a whole lot has changed since then. Like so many old meat shops from that era, it's got not-great fluorescent lighting. It'd be a good set for a Jim Jarmusch movie, or a clip from Jim White's strange but superb documentary about life in the out-of-the-way South, *Searching for the Wrong-Eyed Jesus.* Walk in the front door and you're greeted by a plastic pig holding a "Welcome" sign atop the refrigerated meat case. Another sign nearby proclaims, "Don't see it? Ask!" A third announces, "We accept food stamps."

The walls are pretty much covered with press clippings in various stages of yellowing: an *Atlanta Journal Constitution* article from June 2007 and a *Knoxville News-Sentinel* piece from 10 years earlier were the two that caught my eye out of the 20 or so taped up *au naturel,* or hung on the wall in simple frames. Over in the corner is a five-year-old University of Tennessee football schedule (which would make it 2002—the Vols went up against Wyoming in the season opener that year). There are some handwritten cards and fan letters as well, including a nice old note from the UPS delivery guy, who has probably been on the Benton's route for a long time now. There's also a horseshoe hanging on the wall: every little bit helps when you're curing the old-fashioned way.

To the left of the shop is Allan's office; to the right is the shipping area. The walls in both rooms are dotted with dozens of small pieces of colored paper taped up at random angles. I asked if they were incoming orders. Laughing and shaking his head, the fellow who was showing us around just said, "Allan's got a system."

In between the two rooms is the actual retail space, at the center of which is an old refrigerated deli case that was probably purchased back when the building was built in the 1970s. It's mainly stocked with slices and slabs of Benton's bacon, sliced and whole pieces of his long-cure country hams, and some of Allan's mountain-style smoked sausage. As a sort of nod to one-stop shopping there are also a handful of simple cheeses—nothing fancy, just the sort of stuff you might want to buy a pound of if you lived nearby and were picking up some ham or bacon for sandwiches. On top of the case sit big bottles of sorghum syrup from a mill in Delano (which is down closer to Chattanooga) and smaller jars of sourwood honey, the clear-running, delicately flavored single-blossom honey so justifiably famous in that part of the world. All in all the shop is probably no bigger than the original Deli, which had about 700 square feet of selling space when we opened back in 1982. "In December," Allan explained with a smile, "people are lined up to the door. We hardly have time to sweep the floor."

Walk on out the back of the retail space and you come into the curing and aging area. The bacon slabs and hams hang from well-worn, thick-beamed maple wood racks. The production methods are pretty basic, and have stayed true to what Allan learned from his folks. And while there's a fair bit of pork hanging, it's nowhere near as much as Allan would like: demand is exceeding his supply. At Zingerman's we call this a good problem, but Allan's not very happy about it. In the two days I spent with him and the other SFA folks he must have apologized for shortages 16 times.

I'm glad I got down there to see Allan's place and hear his story. Before I went, I'd really misread the way that Benton's came to be what it is today. Having heard how Allan had started out as a high school guidance counselor and later bought the bacon business from a guy named Albert Hicks, well, I don't want to admit this, but I'd decided that it must have been Hicks who'd gotten the smoking and curing act together, and that Allan then bought the business as one of those second-career moves we see so many of in the food world. Boy, was I wrong.

Mind you, my information wasn't incorrect. But my interpretation sure was. Albert Hicks did indeed start a little smokehouse in the 1940s. He'd been curing hams at his house for years and picked up a bit of a reputation. Remember, this was back in an era when most every farm family in the area was still curing its own hams and bacon. But as folks moved off the land and into cities, demand for country ham that could be bought—not just eaten by the family that cured it—gradually grew.

All this was happening at about the same time Allan was finishing his college degree. While the idea of becoming a guidance counselor initially appealed to him, he quickly realized that the career might not be what he'd hoped. "I looked at the salary schedule and I realized I had made a horrible choice. And then I heard that this fellow, Mr. Hicks, was selling his place, and I went to him and I said 'Would you sell it to me?' And in 1973 he did."

This is where the tale really takes a turn. Modest though he is, this is a story about the patience, persistence, hard work and passion of Allan Benton. Meeting him in person, I quickly realized that curing and smoking was no change-of-career or casual retirement project. It's where he came from. "I was born so far back in the hills of Virginia that you had to look straight up to see the sun," he said. "We were desperately poor even by Appalachian standards. But I didn't know that. Neither side of my family owned an automobile. Neither owned a tractor. They took a gooseneck hoe and they farmed the land like that." He thought for a minute and added, "They actually raised almost everything they ate."

"The pork that I make," he went on, "probably isn't any better than what my parents made. It was done then purely for sustenance. It was a way of life to preserve the meat." Pork was part of everyday eating, but of course people had it at the holidays, too. "My mom and dad moved to Madisonville when I was about two years old. We would go back to the hills of Virginia to visit on the Wednesday before Thanksgiving. Hill people would slaughter, traditionally, on Thanksgiving Day." This last bit caught me a bit by surprise, because the more typical to-slaughter time is usually around Christmas and New Year's. But others confirmed Allan's memory. Up in the mountains, where it's cooler, the animals run out of forage in the fields sooner, and the killing can commence safely because temperatures get down into the thirties by early December.

Purchasing Albert Hicks' smokehouse put Allan back into the world he'd been raised in. Of course he'd never done any curing work professionally, so it took some time for him to translate what he'd learned at home as a kid into what he needed to do to make a living at it. "After six or eight weeks I began to figure out that this is not rocket science. I actually ran that business in Mr. Hicks' back yard for the first four years. I was as guilty as some moonshiner in the hills," he said. "I broke the law every ham I sold." I never saw Allan as the lawbreaking type, but I guess if you put it that way . . . he was a rebel with a country-ham cause. After a bit, Allan began to learn more about pork curing from the staff at the University of Tennessee in Knoxville. "That didn't sit so good with Mr. Hicks," Allan said smiling. "He told me, 'If you listen to those educated fools, you're soon going to be out of business.'" Fortunately, Allan chose to listen to the experts. He gradually blended the hands-on experience of his childhood with what he was learning 40 miles away in Knoxville.

While Benton's bacon and ham may be highly prized today, they hardly got that way overnight. "After we built the building," Allan went on, with a blend of sadness, determination and that sense that what you've believed in has actually been right all along, "I endured all sorts of threats. The nitrate threat. The health conscious movement. The changing lifestyle because people don't go out and cook gravy and biscuits as my mother did." He shook his head. "I mean, the guys who quick-cure these hams can do it so much faster. I tried one batch of those quick-cure hams just to see how it would turn out and it didn't turn out very well. So I determined if I just stick with quality, there would be a market. For the first 25 years I would lay awake at night with knots in my stomach as big as my fist worrying."

Like the small cheesemakers in Wisconsin who stuck it out through the tough times of the 1960s and '70s, Allan hung with his ham and bacon business long enough to see the food world come around to where he'd been all along. John Fleer, who at the time was the chef at Blackberry Farms, helped elevate Allan's country-cured bacon into the culinary limelight. "John tried the bacon and he asked for a delivery a week," Allan recalled. "I said, 'Well you know it's a long ways off the road. I'm going to have to charge you an extra ten cents a pound to make the delivery.'" I had to laugh,

Romance and Regulations

I realize that some of the plants in which these great bacons are made may sound rurally romantic. But just to be clear, while they may not be big in size, and they definitely aren't always that glamorous, all are very closely monitored by the USDA in accordance with government codes for the production of cured meats. So while I love the idea of the characters in Harriette Arnow's essays slaughtering a hog in the hills of Kentucky, or of Allan Benton's mother making bacon out back of their home in the hills of Virginia, please understand that Allan's operation is still outfitted with plenty of stainless steel sinks for sanitizing, and he practices all the safe meat-handling procedures you'd expect (but we don't always get anymore) from bigger plants. If the scale is radically smaller than some Hormel or Oscar Mayer operation, the emphasis on quality and craft is also far higher. And the reality is that there's no one curing bacon for commercial sale that doesn't have to meet those government standards.

as Allan did, when he told me this. "Fortunately, he was willing to pay it. I owe a great debt of gratitude to him—I wouldn't be doing things the way we do today without his help."

I also have to smile because Allan's a reluctant recipient of all the attention. He told the story of his debut at the Southern Foodways Alliance back in 2003. "John T. called me and asked if I'd come down to Oxford for the Symposium," he recounted. "I said I couldn't do it. And he said, 'Allan, you don't know what you're saying no to.' So I agreed to go down there. I said to myself, 'These are people with sophisticated tastes. And I'm going to fry them country ham.' The knot in my stomach has never been so big." As you can tell by now, Allan's a great one for stomach knots, but an even bigger one for pork bellies. Fortunately, everyone loved his bacon—as well they should have.

As we walked through the curing rooms, someone in our small party asked if Benton's brines the pork before they cure it. I tried to hide my shock that the question had even come up: it seems akin to asking a sushi chef if he cooks the fish before serving it. This is *country*—not city—bacon, and a big part of what makes it special is the simple fact that it's cured as long and intensely as it is, *without* water. The man who was showing us around managed to restrain himself and simply shake his head "no," though there was a slight roll of the eyes and a hint of a sardonic smile as he did so.

Sans water, the curing commences shortly after the fresh pork bellies arrive at the plant. Lately Benton's has been moving to buying Berkshire hogs, and that's what we buy from him for Zingerman's. Allan says there's a definite difference in the flavor of the meat. Regardless of the breed, all the slabs get a really good rubdown with brown sugar and salt and are then left to set for about four and a half weeks. When the bacon bellies are done curing the racks are rolled out back into the smoke box. The box can't be more than 12 by 20 feet: big enough to hold a couple of racks of bellies, but that's about it. The bacon gets about 48 hours in the smoker, almost always over hickory. "Heat has a lot to do with it," Allan told me. "You need heat to open up the meat to let it take smoke. We try to keep it at about 85 to 110 [°F] in there," he explained. The length of the cure and the smoke time—both nearly twice what most folks do—are clearly the biggest contributors to the intensity of the flavor. "It's a very intense smoke," Allan kept repeating.

"People either love it or hate it," he added. Which to him, and to me, too, is actually a good thing. "We want to try to make something special." And the bacon is indeed special. In 2007, Allan was honored with the Southern Foodways Alliance's Lifetime Achievement Award. Based on what you now know about the last twenty-odd years of his life, you'll understand that the recognition was well-earned.

"We still have our old family place in Virginia," he volunteered. "It's 175 years old. Tin roof, but the house still stands. The smokehouse is still there. It's a log smokehouse with a dirt floor. They actually homesteaded that property. What I'm doing today is just an extension of what I was doing all my life." Because of Allan Benton's vision—and his dedication and stubbornness in making it a reality—the rest of us get the chance to taste great country-cured bacon much the way it would have tasted a hundred years ago.

A Legion of Bacons of Foreign Origin

While most of the book so far has focused on American bacon, there is of course a whole worldful of, shall we say, "un-American" bacon out there. Rather than lapsing into a stereotypical American tendency to downplay the rest of the world, I wanted to share some of the most interesting of the other styles of cured pork with you here. What follows, then, is a little foray into "foreign" bacons: in particular Hungarian, Italian, Irish, English and Canadian.

Why those five? Well, quite simply, really just because we sell them at Zingerman's, and because they've been an interesting element of the American immigrant experience. That said, there's still a long list of bacons that I haven't even touched here: the classic cured pork of France, Germany, Denmark and probably most every other country of Europe (I've heard that Lithuanians make great bacon buns!). And then there's all the good stuff from the Far East: China, Korea and the other parts of non-Muslim Asia. Apologies to any country whose bacon has been left out. All I can say is that I'm happy to learn more. And I've already started on the sequel, so send me your bacon info! In the meantime, here's an unrepresentative but hopefully engaging look at a few bacons of foreign origin.

Hungarian Double-Smoked Bacon

To say that bacon is an important part of Hungarian cooking is a huge understatement. The more I learn about it, the more I've come to think that in Hungary bacon is . . . well, it's got the power of olive oil in Italy *and* bacon in the U.S. all rolled into one culturally powerful pork cannonball. I haven't been to Hungary yet, but it's very high on my priority list for putting together any sort of Camp Bacon field trips to come; we here in the States are limited in our ability to experience Hungarian bacon because the FDA currently prohibits importation of the authentic article. Fortunately, the long-standing Hungarian immigrant community has been producing good American-made versions for over a century. The 1916 book, *The Hotel Butcher, Garde Manger and Carver,* already listed it among the country's better bacons of the era (though the book adds, parenthetically, that it's "not much relished except by foreigners").

Me being me, drawn to the outsiders and "rejects" of history, this last line makes me want to run right out and buy Hungarian bacon immediately—if "foreigners" relished it, it's likely that anarchists probably were partial to it too. (In those days, the tabloids worked mightily to spin stories about the trouble making of anarchists and others who'd come here from overseas. All of which was exacerbated when Leon Czolgosz, an anarchist of Polish origin, assassinated President William McKinley in 1901. I have no idea if Czolgosz had any affinity for bacon, but I do know that he was the subject of a play published by Eric Schlosser, whom most of you will know better for his now-classic book, *Fast Food Nation.*)

If you find Hungarian bacon in the U.S. today, it has more than likely been made by the Bende family of Chicago. (The name is pronounced "Ben-deh" in Hungarian, but over here they seem to say "BEN-dee," rhyming with "trendy.") Mr. Bende himself—I don't actually know his first name, because every time I call they just refer to him, respectfully and perhaps a bit secretively, as "Mr. Bende"—came over to the States as a young boy with his parents in the fall of 1956, shortly after the failed Hungarian Revolution.

"My father came from a family of butchers and meat processors, and he started to cure the meats after he came here," Mr. Bende explained, in his calm and very measured manner. I was intrigued to learn he came to the States in the aftermath of the Hungarian Revolution. But since we were talking pork, not politics, I shifted my questions to bacon. "What do you use to cure and how long is the curing?" I inquired. "It's a salt dry rub," he responded quietly. Then . . . silence.

I've interviewed a lot of food producers over the years, which is why I knew right then I wasn't going to get very far with Mr. Bende. But I don't give up easily. I tried again, asking this time about the length of the cure. "It's cured for a certain period of time," he said. I waited. So did he. I broke down. "Do you use paprika?" I offered, hoping to enter the conversation through a side door. "No," he said politely, then paused again. "No. We don't use any paprika."

"What about the smoke?" I asked. "I'm curious what type of wood you use, and how long you smoke it for?" "Well," he started out, "some people call it 'double-smoked.'" For a second I thought I'd broken through. "But that doesn't really mean anything," he added. "So much for my subtitle," I thought to myself. Again, I waited. So did he. He won. "So, how long do you smoke for?" I tried. "It's made in the traditional way," he said. "It's smoked until the point at which it's ready."

All I could do was smile. I wondered if Mr. Bende's cryptic responses were a throwback to his family's history on the other side of the Berlin Wall. (Even Communism couldn't diminish Hungarians' passion for pork, however. In 1954, the country issued a stamp

commemorating the 35th anniversary of the Proclamation of the Hungarian Soviet Republic, featuring a Hungarian worker holding a flag with a red sow on it.)

Some of the producers I've talked to over the years . . . I ask them one good question and I get an entire essay's worth of an answer in return. But with Mr. Bende, I think the word-exchange rate topped out at about one of his for every two of mine. If you subtracted from his answers the words that he was merely repeating from my questions I was even further in the hole. All I could do at that point was smile. This was like a conversation out of Kafka's "The Trial." I thought back to my studies of Soviet history. "Double-smoked" might not mean much of anything to Mr. Bende, but I'm guessing that Double-07 certainly would. Mr. Bende's reality seemed like it was anchored in the secrecy and insecurity of the Berlin Wall, baton-wielding border guards, Khrushchev and the KGB, not the openness of twenty-first-century American accessibility going through Google, blogging and Facebook. Given history, his reserve isn't really all that unreasonable. In Communist-controlled Hungary when you said too much to the wrong person, you might well have been sent off to a camp, but it most definitely wasn't one called "Camp Bacon," and you didn't usually get to go home at the end of the summer.

But, hey, nothing to lose. So I continued apace. "How do you like to eat the bacon?" Again, a few seconds of silence. "It can be eaten raw as is," he explained. "It's shaved, more or less." "And what do people eat it with?" He waited a second, then explained what must be exceptionally obvious to someone who's spent his entire life around the product. "With bread. And maybe some onion." "You can cook with it too, right?" "Yes, you can cook with it. My wife uses it in dishes to add flavor."

That was it. I decided to give up with grace rather than antagonize this very gracious, if tight-lipped man. Fortunately, I've subsequently found more voluble sources for information about Hungarian bacon. One is the late George Lang, the great Hungarian-born restaurateur and food writer who opened 300 restaurants in nearly 30 countries during his lifetime, the best-known of which was Manhattan's Café des Artistes. Learning a bit about him, I have the sense that Lang and I have a lot more in common than Mr. Bende and I do. Lang was born Gyorgy Deutsch in 1924 into an academically oriented, Jewish-Hungarian, kosher-keeping home. The family was fairly well off and lived in the easy to remember, very simple to spell (just kidding) town of Szekefehervar, about 35 miles from Budapest. In 1944 the family was sent to a labor camp by the Nazis. His parents died in the camp, but Gyorgy got out and made his way to the U.S in 1946, where he changed his name to George Lang. Given the literal meaning of the surname he'd been born with—"Deutsch" means "German"—it's not that hard to see why he chose to change it. Lang was his mother's maiden name.

Unlike Mr. Bende, Lang loved to talk—and write. His 1971 classic, *The Cuisine of Hungary*, includes dozens of bacon references. In describing life on the Hungary's Great Plains, Lang wrote that "Cognac may be the 'refined lady' most suited to accompany you to an elegant dinner, but on a cold winter morning on the farm, starting the day with a piece of roast bacon and a slice of crusty, toasted bread, you would prefer the peasant beauty of a Hungarian fruit brandy. It would warm you up and give you strength to start the day."

"If you're lucky," he adds, "you'll catch one of the men roasting bacon. It would be hard to find a type of bacon that the Hungarian does not like. As the local saying goes, the breakfast consists of bread with bacon, the lunch is bacon with bread, and the dinner is a combination of the two. . . . Bacon roasting became almost a ritual, with the dogma and formalized customs of a religious ceremony."

Lang enumerates at least a dozen different varieties of Hungarian bacon, ranging from "salted" (what we would call dry-cured) to "smoked," which in turn is broken down into three different sub-categories: bread bacon, fine bacon (*Csemege*) and paprika bacon. Moving down the list, Lang writes about *Abalt*, a bacon that's dry-cured, then pickled in brine and finally either rolled in paprika or very lightly smoked. His list also includes *Kassai* bacon, which is cured in garlic and salt brine, rubbed with beef blood and a lot of paprika, and then smoked, as well as roast bacon: dry-cured pork that has been soaked in milk then fried in a lot of pork fat. The more I read Lang's descriptions, the more I started to think that bacon must be to Hungarians what everyone always says snow is to the Eskimos. Talk about line extensions: I need to get to a Budapest butcher shop and see how this all plays out in real life.

Lang was the one who taught me that the variety we buy from Mr. Bende—dry-cured and "smoked until the point at which it's ready"—is called *Kolozsvari*, *Ciganyszalonna* or *Zigeuner speck* (pronounced *KO-lash-vary*; *si-GAN-y-sha-LOAN-a*; and *zig-OIN-er spek*, respectively—the last two are Hungarian and German, respectively, for "Gypsy bacon"). "Often," Lang explains, "the bones are removed, and the meaty slab will be in one big square piece." This

is exactly what you get when you buy Bende's bacon. As Mr. Bende
said, it comes ready to eat. All you need is a bit of good bread
to go with it: rye is great, but so is a crusty country loaf like the
French Mountain Bread we make at the Bakehouse. In this sense, it
reminds me, both culinarily and culturally, of the cured ham known
as *speck* that comes from the Alto Adige/Sud Tyrol region of northern Italy, part of the Austro-Hungarian Empire until it was annexed
by Italy in 1919 in the aftermath of WWI.

In Hungary people hold pieces of *Koloszvari* over the fire and
catch the drippings on a slice of rye bread, which they eat with the
bacon and some onion, like an inverted version of bacon-fat fon-
due. This is most definitely poor people's food: a small bit of hot
fat adding flavor to dry bread and one of the most basic year-round
vegetables. An acquaintance tells me it's called a *szalonna sutes*—a
bacon cookout. Lang writes about these gatherings in loving detail.
Wood-gathering, fire-building, stick-sharpening, bread-slicing . . .
the *sutes* is no casual event. (It would probably merit its own sum-
mer-long training program at Camp Bacon.) When everything's
ready the cook "cuts off a half pound of bacon in an oblong shape
and puts it on the wooden spit making sure that the end of the stick
does not protrude." I have clear images of Kolozsvari cowboys out
on the plains, horses tied up nearby, each with a *kalap* (the traditional Hungarian hat) pushed back on their head, the perfume of
the bacon filling the cool autumn air.

"It sounds simple?" Lang asks, rhetorically. "Perhaps it is if you
do everything properly. But it's very easy to get a smoky, unpleasant-
tasting bacon, and even easier to drop the bacon into the fire or get
burned with the red-hot, dripping fat. The love of rituals, order, and
a place for everything and everything in its place, helps the Hungarian country folk to make a royal feast out of such simple pleasures as
eating bacon with bread."

Kolozsvari is great for cooking, too. Like Mrs. Bende, I add it to
stews, sauces and soups as a seasoning. I also like it in bean salads,
or fried and mixed into scrambled eggs—a little bit goes a long way.
It's great for making traditional Hungarian potato salad, as well:

just fry small pieces until crisp, then remove them from the pan. In the fat that's left behind, gently cook some chopped sweet onion until soft. Add a little flour and stir until smooth, then add a bit of vinegar and sugar and cook for a few minutes until you have a smooth dressing. Pour the dressing over some just-cooked potatoes and sprinkle on the bacon pieces. Add a good dash of Hungarian paprika, then eat it while it's hot. It's delicious. Lang also lists a nice little recipe for "Vinegary Bacon Soup": bits of bacon fried with onion and paprika, then added to beef stock finished with a good dose of vinegar. Or you can toss the bacon drippings onto vegetables as a salad dressing—again, with some high-quality Hungarian paprika for good measure.

On a grander scale, the great chef Louis Szathmary—who, like Mr. Bende, was born in Hungary and later landed in Chicago—used to use Hungarian bacon in his venison ragout. He fried the bacon along with onions, garlic and mushrooms that had first been sautéed in lard, then simmered with a bit of tomato juice and red wine. The exact recipe is reprinted in James Vilas' *Bacon Cookbook*.

Anyone with Hungarian roots is likely to know a fair bit about this bacon. But outside the ethnic community few people seem to be aware of it. Hopefully this book will help get the secret out. Buy a bit and help put Mr. Bende's Kolozsvari on the culinary map.

Warning—Lean Loins May Not be Sufficiently Lascivious: A Trio of Anglo-Irish Offerings

I have to tell you that these next three bacons, all of which have British roots, are unlike the bacon most of you grew up eating. All three are delicious, and legions of super-loyal fans get as excited about eating them as any American bacon fanatic might be about

Benton's, Broadbent's or Burgers'. All are very definitely bacon. Just be aware that they're . . . well . . . *different.*

While American bacons, which are made by curing and (usually) smoking fatty pork bellies, tend toward a luxurious smokiness, the British, Irish and Canadian versions are more understated. A stiff upper lip, maybe, compared to their wilder western cousins? All three are made from pork loin, so for starters they're much leaner than their belly-based American brothers. And all are brine-cured but not smoked. I don't want to delude an innocent bacon loving American who's never "been abroad" (at least in bacon terms) into thinking you're headed down some devilishly rich, dietary path of sin when what you're getting here is really much leaner and, to my taste, not as sensual as the stuff you're used to getting so supremely excited about.

Of course, that said, I don't think any warning on a box or a book ever stopped anyone from smoking or any other gently mis-guided behavior so I'm guessing—and hoping—you'll keep reading (and eating) regardless. These bacons may not quite be the beasts you're used to but they're darned good and worth getting to know. So on we go.

Wiltshire Cut British Bacon

While bacon is way out front in Hungarian cuisine, in Britain it tends to sit silently and steadfastly, usually next to a pair of fried eggs, a bit of fried tomato and slices of white toast. Which is why I suppose I never paid British bacon all that much mind. I've never been a big breakfast eater, and since we weren't able to import it into the U.S. and I wasn't aware of any noteworthy Stateside produc-ers, British bacon remained very low on my list of interests.

At least until I stumbled onto the Wiltshire Cut, or, as it's also known, the Wiltshire Cure. If I hadn't seen it mentioned in a book about bacon I probably would have assumed Wiltshire Cut was a brand of loose-leaf tobacco. Half a year and a whole lot of learning later, I've completely changed my mind about British bacon. It's going to have to be a central element of the summer program at Camp Bacon.

I first read about the Wiltshire Cut in George J. Nicholls' 1917 book, *Bacons and Hams*. "The Wiltshire-cut side is the kind of bacon which is most generally sold in London and in the south of England," he writes. "It is the whole side of the hog, including both ham or gammon and shoulder." This description didn't exactly excite my interest the first time I read it—Nicholls' stereotypically British reserve and fondness for technical details blunted the impact. The book is mostly about unglamorous subjects like gross margins, payment terms, fore-ends, fore-hocks, and the minutiae of pork-cutting. About the headiest prose you'll find in his work comes at the end of the introduction, where he shares that, "The London cheesemonger of 1560 sold [bacon and ham] in his shop just as his successor does over 350 years later, and equally with him he had to take care that his bacon was sound and free from blemish. The penalty then was more drastic, perhaps, as the record of a cheesemonger of the former year shows, who was being charged with selling 'measlle' bacon, and convicted was compelled to ride about London on horseback with his face to the tail, and then was placed in the pillory with two large chunks of the offending bacon hung over his head, a notice being appended that he had been twice caught in the same misdemeanor!!" Racy stuff by turn-of-the-century British standards.

Let's just say that George Nicholls and Sarah Katherine Lewis are coming from opposite ends of the personality spectrum. And yet it's easy enough to see a bit of Lewis' spirit reflected in Nicholls' book dedication: "written not for the general reader but for him whose business it is to purvey the toothsome rasher." I guess the love for bacon unites people from all walks of life—even stuffy British scholars of pork butchery and racy, food-loving former sex workers.

As you know all too well by now, I'm far more prone than the typical human to pursuing historical obscurities. Still, I tucked Wiltshire Cut away in some dusty corner of my mind for a rainy day. The world wasn't going to let it rest there for long, however. Although I'd spent 30 years in the food business without hearing much about the Wiltshire Cut, it suddenly started coming up everywhere.

The whole scenario was one of those six degrees of connection stories that seem to come up so often these days (I prefer the positive "degrees of connection" to the more-common "degrees of separation"). It started while I was sampling some very good Canadian bacon from the Real Canadian Bacon Company. For reasons I couldn't quite figure out, all their print materials described the product as "Wiltshire Cure." Canadian bacon is pretty well-known in the States, whereas "Wiltshire Cure" is so obscure that even a food-business veteran like me had barely heard of it. So I asked RCBC founder Ken Haviland why he'd used the name. He explained that since Canadian bacon had originated from the Wiltshire Cure, and since he was trying to undo people's conception of Canadian bacon as strictly a breakfast food, it seemed like a logical choice. (You can almost imagine Edward Bernays launching a "Take the Cure" ad campaign to persuade overstressed Americans that eating real Canadian bacon will make them more like their calmer northern neighbors . . .)

So I decided to look a little deeper into the Wiltshire Cut. I learned that it was created by the Harris family from the town of Calne, in southeastern England, during the mid-nineteenth century. So I went back to George Nicholls' book, and discovered that the Harris family was mentioned there, as well. I just hadn't known to watch for them in my earlier readings.

Since I was calling him anyways, I asked my friend Randolph Hodgson from Neal's Yard Dairy in London about it on the phone one morning. His area of expertise is cheese, not pork, but it never hurts to ask, right? He surprised me by saying that he thought William Tullberg—a man whom we'd both known for a good 20 years from his very good line of mustards produced under the Wiltshire Tracklements label—had once worked with that very same Harris family.

If nothing else, the geography was right—both were from Wiltshire. So I tracked William down, first on email, then by phone. I quickly discovered that he knew all about the Harrises, the Wiltshire Cut, and numerous other aspects of British pork-curing. Wiltshire, I learned from William, has a pork tradition dating back hundreds of years. In fact, the name of the biggest town in the county—Swindon—comes from "Swin down," meaning Swine Hill, a reference to the fact that hogs used to graze there centuries ago. Wiltshire, it turns out, is home to a whole lot of oak forests. So there, as in western Spain, hogs were finishing their eating careers on acorns, enhancing the flavor of the finished pork. As it happens, Wiltshire is also just east of Somerset, home of Cheddar cheese, which meant a lot of whey was also available for feeding the hogs.

Wiltshire's pork prominence grew in modern times because it lay on the droving road from Bristol, where huge numbers of imported Irish hogs were being landed, to London, where they were slaughtered. Calne became the capital of British pork curing—the UK's own Porkopolis. Calne was also home to the Harris family, who founded their bacon business in about 1770. The family firm was apparently quite successful until the late 1840s, when the potato famine led to a crash in their regular supply of Irish hogs. Looking for new sources of pork, Mr. Harris traveled to the U.S. While he was unable to devise a way to transport American pigs back to Calne, his visit did expose him to the new techniques of high-tech temperature management ("temperature control" would be an overstatement) that were becoming popular here. Americans had learned to pack ice on the roof of a structure and use fans to circulate the cooled air. And, thus, in 1856, the Wiltshire Cure was conceived.

The cooler temperatures made possible by this early refrigeration system allowed Harris to cure his pork for longer, which, in turn, enabled him to use less salt. It also freed him and his fellow producers in the warmer climes of southern England to work safely through the summer's heat. Unlike the older style, dry-cured bacons, Wiltshire Cure was done in a brine of water, salt and saltpeter for three to four days and then taken to the curing rooms to rest for another 10. The result is a mellow, meaty bacon. And because it's cut from the loin with the tail left on, Wiltshire, like its Irish and Canadian cousins, has a lot less fat than "streaky" American bacon.

The Wiltshire Cut became so popular in the late nineteenth century that new railway lines were routed through Calne, so that hogs could be off-loaded at the Harris factory and finished bacon could be shipped on to London and points beyond. I find it ironic, or at least curious, that the railroads put the drovers out of business by following the paths that they had walked with their pigs for hundreds of years. The Harris factory had closed in 1983, and from what I've heard Calne is now a rather grim place to live.

By now, though, our conversation had piqued my historian's instincts. So I decided to Google "William Tullberg bacon" to find out a bit more. Again, one coincidence led to another. The first hit on my search list was something called "William's Pork." Only half paying attention (I was probably doing five other things at the same time), I assumed "William" must be a British producer of old-style back bacon. But when I clicked over to his site, I discovered that I had actually found a British-*style* bacon being made and sold in the unlikely location of Lumberton, North Carolina. That caught my attention: not only was Wiltshire Cut being made in in the U.S., but it sounded like this mysterious William was making it in a way that was right up our artisanal alley. The website quoted from all sorts of good reviews. And, better still, because William's Pork was being produced here at home, we'd actually be able to get it without flying all the way to Britain for breakfast.

Now, once I get going my patience dissipates quickly. I mean, I'd been just fine knowing nothing about Wiltshire Cure for three decades. But, suddenly, after a few minor coincidences, I just had to learn more about it *immediately*. Unfortunately, by this time it was already early on a Thursday evening. On the odd chance that William worked the same sort of late hours that I do, I called the company number. I got their voice mail, which meant I was going to have wait until morning to learn more, and even longer to actually taste the bacon (being in the mail order business myself, I knew there was no way they'd be able to ship me samples before Monday). It's not like I couldn't sleep (I can always sleep!) but I was definitely driven to learn more. At least the woman's voice on the phone message had betrayed a decidedly English accent, so I figured I was onto something authentic.

At nine the next morning I promptly picked up the phone and dialed North Carolina. The woman who answered sounded like the same one whose voice I'd heard the night before. She suggested that I talk to William, and offered to take a message. When he left me a return voicemail later that day, I was caught completely off-guard: the bacon might be British, but William's accent was North Carolina all the way.

When I finally caught up with the elusive William Johnson, I learned that he was an accountant who first encountered British bacon during the dozen or so years he and his English wife (the woman on the phone) had lived in the UK. The couple moved to North Carolina in the 1990s, and, unsurprisingly, couldn't find Wiltshire Cut at their corner grocery. So, in one of those later-in-life entrepreneur stories that are so common in the food business, William decided he'd try learn how to make bacon the way they did it in England. He traveled back to Britain to study bacon making with a farmer there, then spent the next two years trying to get the recipes right.

Because no one in North Carolina had any experience with the techniques he'd learned, William actually found himself training the local slaughterhouse to cut the loins he needed. He and his wife then cure them in a brine of water, salt, sugar and touch of nitrite. They do a longer cure than most—seven to 10 days—to allow for more flavor development. The result is a raw product that needs to be cooked gently before serving. While you can certainly consume it any way you like, 97 percent of the time it's going to be plated up with that classic British breakfast of fried eggs, fried tomatoes and toast. If you really want to get your morning off to a flying start, you can even fry the bread in the bacon fat, too.

By the time I "found" him, William's Pork had already been producing highly regarded Wiltshire-style bacon for a good seven or eight years. Both British Airways and Virgin Atlantic serve it to their first class passengers on U.S.-to-UK flights. But I have to I admit the whole thing caught me by surprise. I'm fairly up to speed on the American specialty-food world, and had been researching bacon for a good two years. So I have no idea how I'd missed Wiltshire Cut and William's Pork. I'm glad I found them, though. My curiosity about what I had thought to be a nearly irrelevant sidenote had turned up a product worthy of selling at Zingerman's. We were finally in a position to help people in the U.S. enjoy a good, traditional British breakfast.

Old-Style English Bacon and the Staffordshire Way to Start the Day

While most folks who know British bacon today have eaten Wiltshire Cut, only a minority will have had a chance to savor the older-style, dry-cured British recipes. Fortunately there are a handful of producers in the UK still doing this traditional curing. My sampling has been anything but scientific, but so far I've most enjoyed the version made by Melvin Ling in the small city of Shrewsbury, in the northwest English county of Shropshire.

Melvin's mentor in curing is Maynard Davies, the main man of British bacon and the author of one of my favorite books on the subject of pork, *Adventures of a Bacon Curer.* Maynard wanted to make sure his recipes wouldn't be lost after his retirement, so he offered to share them with Melvin, whose work he had admired at

Cooking with British Bacon

Like the Irish, the Brits love bacon and cabbage (*not* corned beef and cabbage—see page 110). In *Delizie: The Epic History of the Italians and Their Food,* author John Dickie mentions that nineteenth-century Italian cooks were trained to make the dish in order to appeal to the ever-growing number of English tourists, who sadly had no taste for the local cuisine. Peter Vaughan, who co-owns a shop called The Healthy Life in the town of Devizes, offers a very simple recipe: core and slice a good cabbage, then drop it into boiling water for half a minute or so to soften it. Meanwhile, fry some British bacon until soft, add the cabbage, and stir well. Throw in a generous sprinkling of caraway seed and cook it all for 15 minutes, or longer, until the cabbage is done to your liking.

Melvin's cheese and specialty food shop, Appleyards, located on Wyle Cop in the center of Shrewsbury. Selling from Appleyards, as well as through his stand at the local market, Melvin has produced an exceptional range of bacons. But he gives credit where credit is due: "Maynard's the god of bacon," he said with only the hint of a smile. "He taught me everything I know."

Thin, of medium height with thinning gray hair, Melvin looks a bit professorial in his long white butcher's coat and rimless glasses, which he wears a little low on his nose. He's quite passionate about his pork curing, though in a very low-key way. "You're only as good as the last bacon you produce," he proffered with Maynard-like modesty, "and you never quite know what will come next."

Melvin is currently curing about a dozen different sorts of bacon, nearly all of them from Maynard's recipes. He starts with pork exclusively from female pigs, which he believes is more tender. (Many bacon producers do use males, but only if they've been castrated. As Sam Edwards quipped, "Balls on boars make for funky tasting meat.") He also works only with hogs of heirloom origin: Gloucester Old Spots, Middle Whites and Durocs. Most of his dozen or so bacons (though not quite all) are unsmoked, long dry cures in the British tradition. Since you can't taste his work here in the States, I'll spare you the descriptions and just note that my personal favorites were the Settler's bacon (best I can tell it's cured with salt and brown sugar) and the Staffordshire Black. The latter is a local recipe that Melvin learned from Maynard: dry-cured back and belly (the two together are what the British call "long back") done up over a period of weeks with salt, honey and black treacle, the English equivalent of blackstrap molasses. The end result is a soft, sweet, well-rounded and notably treacly flavor that leads me to think of this as "the Balsamic of bacons." It's Melvin's top seller, which isn't surprising given its local roots. It's also the basis of a traditional Staffordshire breakfast, which you can still find if you visit the northwest of England. As Bob Coleman of Neal's Yard Dairy in London described it, the breakfast is "basically just a fry-up on an oatcake." Which seems about as helpful as describing a really good bagel with smoked salmon and cream cheese as "fish on a roll."

So, for those less familiar with it, to make a Staffordshire breakfast you take a hot Staffordshire oatcake, butter it, then lay on cooked Staffordshire Black bacon, a freshly fried egg and crumbled or grated Cheshire cheese. Because Staffordshire oatcakes are cooked on a griddle, not baked, they're more like thick, eight-inch-diameter tortillas or crepes than the crunchy oatcakes we're used to from Scotland and Ireland: the Staffordshire breakfast comes out as something akin to a British breakfast burrito. It's not hard to see why this would appeal to workers heading out early into the dark,

gray and damp Staffordshire morning. The soft texture and nutti-
ness of the hot oatcake, the meatiness of the bacon and the creami-
ness of the just-cooked egg, all enhanced by the cheese, make for a
pretty good start to a bacon-eater's day.

Canadian Peameal Bacon

Like the Wiltshire Cut, Canadian bacon is a pickled eye of pork loin.
Unlike Wiltshire, the Canadian version retains the tail of the loin,
and after being cured is then, surprisingly to the uninitiated, rolled
in cornmeal. While cornmeal coating is a fairly common technique
for American foods like catfish and clam bellies, as far as I can tell
what the Canadians call "peameal" is a completely unique product
in the bacon world. It's also quite delicious.

From what I've learned, the rolling in meal wasn't a big brilliant
culinary idea, but just a practical solution to a practical problem.
"In the olden days you would go to the grocery store and ask the
man at the meat counter for your 'peameal bacon,'" Canadian-born
bacon importer Ken Haviland told me. "They would grab a hook,
pull a loin out of the brine solution, roll it in cornmeal, package it
up, weigh it, sticker it and hand it to you." That makes sense, as far
as it goes. But the term "peameal" struck me as a bit odd. All the
Canadian bacon I'd ever come across was rolled in cornmeal, so why
wasn't the stuff called "cornmeal bacon"? The answer, apparently,
is that Canadian bacon was originally rolled in ground dried yellow
peas, a coating that was later abandoned in favor of more readily
available cornmeal.

Folks from Canada and some areas on the U.S. side of the border are pretty darned passionate about Canadian bacon—as
passionate in their way as Southerners are about grits. Just talk to
a couple of Canadians or close-to-Canada Americans and you'll
discover that peameal bacon sandwiches are their equivalent of

pastrami in Manhattan or cheese-
steaks in Philadelphia, so much so that
"iconic" is almost an understatement.

Molly Stevens, author of *All About
Braising*, grew up in Buffalo. "In my
family, for some reason, it's long
been one of those ritual foods," she
explained. "Peameal for us symbolizes summer at the
beach in Canada, and all that goes with it; long days, no school,
and so on. I remember one year when an in-law sliced it too thinly,
and we were all silently horrified. Of course, we were polite enough
but each made a mental note to watch the next time that THAT
brother-in-law went anywhere near the peameal. Then there was the
other time when someone bought the pre-sliced stuff. Again, hor-
ror." Her story reminded me of the *jamon serrano* producer in Spain
who once told me, half-smiling, that he'd have to kill me if I cut the
fat off his ham.

Now that we've shuffled the incompetent in-laws safely aside,
where they can't do any damage, how do you serve Canadian bacon?
"The deal is, you get a big hunk—anywhere from two to three
pounds, slice it not too thin, not too thick," Molly said. "Grill it over
medium heat so it stays just ever so pink in the center and the cornmeal coating and external fat grills up crispy. Then you serve it on a
soft sort of Kaiser roll—the best of them have a thin crispy crust and
soft absorbent interior. You slather on Hellmann's mayonnaise, add
lettuce and slices of summer-ripe tomato. Depending on the size of
the roll, who sliced the peameal, your pigginess, etc. you may stack
two slices, or maybe one. Oh, and a few thin slices of orange Canadian cheddar would be acceptable, too."

To my experience, the best Canadian bacon in the States is the
stuff imported by the Real Canadian Bacon Company, based not
far from Ann Arbor in Troy, Michigan. The company was started by
Ken Haviland, who relocated from Ontario to work as an engineering manager at a Michigan auto parts plant. Ken grew increasingly

frustrated that he couldn't find the real Canadian bacon he'd grown up with: most of what's available in the U.S. is already cooked and sometimes smoked and not at all what folks who love the real thing are seeking (I guess we really should refer to it as "American Canadian bacon").

So Ken decided he'd have to import his own. The RCBC offers the peameal both as a big chunk and pre-sliced. In keeping with Molly's advice, I'd recommend going with the chunk and cutting your own. Like her, I prefer it cut a bit thicker—you get a nicer mouth-feel and the eating experience is, I think, more interesting. The flavor is mellow, like a light, refreshing local summer wine compared to the earthy, smoky well-aged intensity of, say, Allan Benton's dry-cured bacon. In fact, now that I think about it the wine analogy fits perfectly with Molly's memories of beach eating. I've made up a fair few sandwiches just as she described them and they really are very nice, refreshing and fun. I cooked the bacon in a skillet, but of course doing it on the grill would be a great way to go.

Incidentally, another good source for peameal—Gord's Great Canadian Bacon—is also located here in Michigan. We're close to Canada, so I guess it makes sense.

Irish Bacon

"The Irish frequently use food and drink as an excuse for talking. This does not mean that the fare is not good, because, in my perhaps biased opinion, Limerick bacon and fresh butter are superior to any other I have eaten elsewhere."

—Ulick O'Connor, in his preface to Rosalind Cole's
Of Soda Bread and Guinness

Like the Wiltshire Cure and Canadian bacon, most Irish bacon today is made from pork loin brine-cured with salt, sugar and spices. Anyone who's been to Ireland knows that it's pretty hard to avoid. Truth is, a lot of Irish people will look askance if you try. I know, because not being a big morning eater I've often tried to turn down a "proper Irish breakfast" in favor of tea and toast. Note that I say "tried"—at least half the time I end up wilting under my host's glare and eating my bacon like a good Irishman should.

This is no small breakfast we're talking about: alongside your rashers you'll often find sausage (sometimes black "puddings," sometimes white, sometimes both on the same plate), tomatoes or mushrooms fried in bacon fat, eggs and toast. And thick, pan-fried slices of bacon—known as "rashers"—are the key. To quote Malachi McCormick's classic *In Praise of Irish Breakfasts*, "It is beyond disputing that bacon is the *ne plus ultra* of the Irish Breakfast. While its tangy intensity draws out the best in many other 'breakfast elements,' it is fair to say that for some of them it is indispensable. Fried field mushrooms become magical in its presence; unbaconed calves liver is unthinkable; the unaccompanied egg, inconceivable."

And lest Americans think of the morning toast as slices of white bread lightly browned in a pop-up toaster, consider this statement

from Florence Irwin's 1949 book *Irish Country Recipes*: "Wheaten or soda bread fried in the pan almost go with bacon and eggs without saying. After the bacon and eggs are cooked, if necessary, extra dripping is put in the pan and all made smoking hot. The neatly cut pieces of home-made bread are very quickly browned on both sides in this and served on the

dish with the bacon and eggs." If all of that isn't enough to fill you up, porridge is usually part of the plan, too. This "morning" meal can also be a great way to end a long evening. As one Irish friend told me, "Of course, it's particularly good after you've had a few pints!"

Not only do the Irish eat a lot of bacon and eggs, Irish legend actually lays claim to having invented the dish. In *Irish Country Recipes*, Irwin tells the tale of an old Irish peasant woman frying her husband's morning bacon in a skillet over the peat fire. Her hens were roosting above the hearth, on the beams where the couple smoked their hams, and on this particular morning one hen knocked an egg out of her nest. The egg hit the pan, cracked and cooked alongside the bacon, so the woman served the two foods to her husband together. He loved the combination so much he ran off to the nearby monastery to tell the monks. (I have to smile— only in Ireland would you run off to tell the monks about your great breakfast discovery!) "And so," Ms. Irwin says, "the fame of the dish penetrated the monastery walls, and from monastery to monastery it spread, and from land to land, and from peoples to peoples, and was relished by rich and poor alike, and all by the grace of God and the irregular proclivities of the lazy old hen." Hey, I'm sure that's *exactly* how bacon and eggs was discovered. Edward Bernays, eat your heart out!

What we know for sure is that bacon has played a prominent role in Celtic cooking and culture for many centuries. While butter is certainly the dominant fat of the island, and potatoes have played their lead role in Irish cooking ever since the explorers brought them back from the New World in the mid-seventeenth century, bacon bridges the gap between ancient Celtic cultures and modern-day Irish cooking. Pigs were already popular 12 centuries ago— their bones account for about a third of the remains found at early Christian burial sites, and there are many ancient accounts of curing and smoking pork. The early Celtic hogs were very likely bony by modern standards, but they were as critical a part of Irish eating in that era as they are today. A prosperous farmer was one who had more than one pig, and land leases often figured a "flitch" or two of bacon into the payments.

Early Irish Farming, by Fergus Kelly, is a fantastic 700-page tome that's subtitled *A Study Based Mainly on the Law-texts of the 7th and 8th Centuries AD.* Given that it's Volume Four of the Early Irish Law Series, I don't think Showtime is likely to make it into a movie anytime soon. So I'll just say that *Early Irish Farming* is . . . well . . . it's a sort of hybrid of the Talmud and the old American *Foxfire* books. It

Grand Little Anecdote

Malachi McCormick, who grew up in Mitchelstown in the north of County Cork, shared his own Irish bacon memory with me. "My grandparents always would have a flitch of bacon hanging up in the chimney. Of course the fire would have been peat. My God that was the best of stuff! . . . My grandmother was a great fan of the bacon. My mother told me once that her mother said to her, just musing in a conversation, 'Isn't the pig a grand little animal?'"

provides you, for instance, with important information about what percentage of the meat from a family's pig a divorced wife should get as part of the settlement. (The answer is two thirds, in case it comes up.) The book also describes how to build the stone-lined pits, called *ulacht fiadh*, that the ancient Celts cooked in. And it gives almanac-like information on which years were particularly good for acorn crops. Apparently 1038 was a very good year! Kelly explains that the seventh-century "wisdom text" *Audacht Morainn* advises readers about guilt by reminding them that the pig's "fat side" has the power to free every face from shame. Some ideas never grow old.

For centuries the Irish raised their hogs from winter through August, feeding them on the "leavings" from the family table, along with grain as well as milk and curd from cheesemaking (not just leftover whey, as was done elsewhere, but actual milk and curd). In autumn, the animals were let loose to forage in the forest. Farmers' stock mingled while munching on wild grasses and tree masts, but each family retained the rights to its own animals. As Brid Mahon explains in *Land of Milk and Honey*, the slaughter began on Martin-mas (November 11) and was limited to months with an "r" in their names. This is one of those folkways that's easy to understand: you really wouldn't want to put up meat during the heat of May, June, July or August if you planned to eat it months or even years later.

Interestingly, finishing pigs on acorns, a practice most commonly associated with Spain, turns out to have been big in Ireland, as well. Quoting from the old records, Kelly writes that the acorn "serves to fatten up the young pigs for immediate killing or to provide them with reserves to survive the hungry days of the coming winter." In what qualified as my favorite lesson of the week, he also notes that a lost opportunity was referred to as "a pig which dies before the acorn-crop." As in modern-day Spain, where the *bellota* (that is, acorn) *Iberico* is by far the highest grade of cured ham, acorn-eating hogs had a special name in Gaelic, *muca for mesruth*.

By 1800, it had become the norm to feed pigs primarily on potatoes, supplemented with milk. (It would be interesting to find out what potato-fed pork tastes like, contrasted, say, with meat from the peanut-fed pigs of Virginia.) In the first half of the nineteenth century, British demand for Irish bacon grew rapidly: whereas about 6,000 pigs were being shipped from Cork each year in the early decades of the century, the number rose to 36,000 by 1820 and to 90,000 by the 1830s. When the Famine hit, the problem affected pigs almost as much as people. According to the historian Peter Foynes in *The Great Famine in Skibbereen*, pigs were pushed to market ever more quickly in order to raise cash. "In fact, one of the recognized signs of increasing food scarcity coming into the winter of 1845," Foynes writes, "was the five fold increase in the number of pigs sent to market in Cork, though it was noted that the pigs were underfed."

While most of the bacon served in Irish restaurants and homes today is brine-cured, dry-curing has a place in the country's culinary traditions, as well. Darina Allen, founder of the Ballymaloe Cookery School south of Cork City, a prolific cookbook author, television host, teacher and champion of traditional food, organic agricul-

Bacon and Oats

According to Mrs. Irwin, author of *Irish Country Recipes,* the dish known in Northern Ireland as *dugan* or in Gaelic as *mealie greachie* was popular among farm laborers from North and North-East Antrim at harvest time. The dish is made from dry oatmeal toasted in bacon fat, with or without the addition of fried onions. According to some it can be topped with a fried egg. A wholly different way to eat oatmeal from what we're used to, but a quite delicious Irish cousin to the Native American blend of oats and bacon.

ture, Slow Food and her own family, shares a recipe for dry-cured bacon in her book, *Traditional Irish Cooking.* It calls for rubbing fresh pork loin with salt and treacle and then letting it age for four weeks before hanging it to dry. Interestingly, the dry-cure recipe dates to 1851, just a few years after the shortage of Irish hogs drove Mr. Harris of Calne to visit the States—a trip that resulted in the wet Wiltshire Cure which now dominates Irish and English bacon-making.

Fingal Ferguson, who makes very good dry- and wet-cured bacons, as well as a very fine farmhouse cheese known as Gubbeen, out at the far southwestern tip of County Cork, told me that the wet cure originated when Irish farmers took their pigs to slaughter and then put the pork into barrels of salt. Later they'd take the meat out and soak it in preparation for use. The curers used saltpeter instead of the more modern nitrite.

Fingal's own bacon begins with fresh pork from old breeds of hogs—Durocs, Tamworths and Saddlebacks—that the family raises on the farm. To my knowledge they're one of only a few producers who both raise the hogs and cure the bacon for sale on the same farm. I don't know of anyone in the U.S. that's doing this on a commercial scale. His hogs are fed the whey from the cheesemaking as well as grains and some leavings from other organic producers in the area, and roam freely on pasture. For his wet cure he uses a recipe from one of Jane Grigson's excellent cookbooks that includes wine and herbs. He also does a dry cure in which the pork loin is rubbed with salt, sugar, herbs and spices, and then matured for a month.

Unfortunately we can't get Fingal's bacon here (there are only a handful of European bacon-makers who pay for the required USDA approval), so you'll have to invest in a trip to Ireland or Great Britain to try it. We do have access to two very good brine-cured Irish bacons in the States, however. The first is from an Irish-owned firm in New York State called Tommy Maloney's. The company came into being in 1920 in County Limerick, and is now run by the fourth generation of Maloneys. "We're the only ones that have Irish bacon made from Irish pigs," says their sales manager, Brendan Keyes. "We do our curing here but the pigs are real Irish." It's significant that the firm's owners and their hogs are from Limerick: Limerick is to Irish bacon what Bordeaux is to French wine. As the late, great Flann O'Brien once wrote, "I have peerless Limerick rashers, and there will be no shortage of that aperitif." The other good Stateside source for Irish bacon is the Irish-owned Shannon Valley Foods, based in Santa Clara, California. They make brine-cured Irish bacon, as well. Both Maloney's and Shannon Valley are quite good, and both will sell you your choice of pre-sliced rashers or chunks for making a classic bacon and cabbage.

You read that right: it's bacon and cabbage that seems to be the truly Irish tradition, *not* corned beef and cabbage. While the Irish themselves aren't in 100 percent consensus on the issue, most of the people I've talked to stand with Malachi McCormick, who asked "What if, this year, you were to dispense with the imposterous dinner of corned beef (it is not a traditional Irish dish) and dispense instead our High Irish Breakfast?" As Maloney's sales manager Brendan Keyes said, "I never had corned beef in my life until I came to this country. In Ireland it was always, bacon and cabbage, never corned beef." Most every Irish cookbook I've found offers two or three recipes for bacon and cabbage. Only the American-Irish cookbooks call for corned beef.

Corned Beef on Rye in Ireland

If you're in Dublin and crave a corned beef sandwich, they bake a very decent Jewish rye at Bretzel Bakery, just a short walk from Dublin's excellent little Jewish museum.

No one can say exactly how corned beef came to replace bacon in this traditional dish. One explanation holds that Irish and Jewish immigrants to the U.S. lived in close quarters. Not being able to get their usual bacon, the Irish arrivals adapted to using the Jews' corned beef instead. It's a good story, but hard to swallow given that we know pork was available even in the poor immigrant neighborhoods of turn-of-the-century America, and it certainly wouldn't have been that hard to brine-cure it for bacon.

Historian Peter Foynes doubts the veracity of the whole Irish bacon versus American corned beef dichotomy. "Corned beef and cabbage," he writes, "in my opinion, is perfectly traditional. I think the apparent disparity arises from the fact that spiced beef, which is a variant of corned beef, was probably associated mainly with the port cities: Cork, Waterford and Dublin, at least. I imagine it was not associated with rural areas. Hence the presence of the two traditions."

Whether it's the only true Irish tradition or just one of several, give bacon and cabbage a try. You won't regret it.

There's a lot more to Irish bacon cookery than just cabbage. Consider Dublin coddle, for example. This less-known but equally classic recipe is basically lots of bacon cooked with potatoes, onions, sausages, salt, pepper and parsley in pork stock or water for many hours. There are hundreds of different versions. Most cooks fry the bacon and sausage first, then mix them with the other ingredients and cook the whole concoction for at least two hours in the oven or atop the stove. It's a simple dish, so the quality of the ingredients makes a big difference. James Joyce was apparently a big fan. Most Dubliners have some story of it, and most will probably tell you it's best with a pint of Guinness (although that's probably true for any dish you ask them about). Because it can be cooked ahead, coddle is quite popular for funerals (seriously) and is often served at the wake. It's also popular as a Sunday night dinner—the sort of comfort food you want before going back to work on Monday morning.

Peter Foynes shared the following story. "My late mother was from Dublin . . . It was the tradition in Dublin to have a fried breakfast on Sunday morning . . . The bacon, which was streaky, was not bought ready-sliced, but whole and then cut as needed. The coddle was a *mixem gatherem* stew made on Saturday night from the scrap bacon, sausage and any other bits and pieces, and was consumed by the men on their return from the pub."

Three More "Bacons" from the Boot: Bellies, Backs and Jowls in the Italian Style

Pancetta

Pancetta is an Italian bacon: an unsmoked pork belly cured with salt and spices, then rolled and aged. Diced and fried, it adds flavor to all types of savory dishes. But what few Americans realize is that the number one way to eat pancetta in Italy is actually raw, as a staple of the antipasto plate alongside prosciutto and salami, maybe some good olives and sticks of fresh fennel. While most of the pancetta sold in America isn't made with this kind of eating in mind, it's what you'll get in any good food setting in Italy. Fortunately that's changing—high-quality pancetta is now being made here in North America.

Traveling in the southern Italian region of Calabria not long ago, I was served some pancetta Calabrese—cured pork belly spiced (as is most everything in the region) with ground red chiles. I took a couple slices off the buffet, unsure what it would be like. Even knowing that it was supposed to be eaten uncooked, I still sort of paused when presented with raw bacon. But damn, it was good. Seriously melt in your mouth, long flavor, deliciously good. The experience reinforced how much I needed to refocus my own pancetta perspective—if you do the same, there's good eating to be had.

And if you do eat it raw, take note that, as with cured hams, longer aging likely means more developed flavor. I learned this from Herb Eckhouse, whose Iowa-made La Quercia pancetta we use at Zingerman's. Like me, Herb grew up in a Jewish home in suburban Chicago. Like me, he went off to college and studied subjects that had nothing in particular to do with food—in his case political science, economics and history.

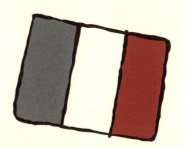

From there our stories diverged onto very different paths. While I got a job washing dishes, Herb went on to work for Pioneer Hi-Bred, the Iowa seed company founded in 1926 by the liberal visionary Henry Wallace. Wallace later became Franklin Roosevelt's Secretary of Agriculture, then his vice president and finally his Secretary of Commerce before running for president himself on the Progressive Party ticket in 1948. Although Pioneer was sold to DuPont in the late 1990s, its original business philosophy and approach to seeds and agriculture were very much aligned with the ideas espoused by many of us on the progressive end of the food world today.

In 1985 Herb was offered the chance to take over Pioneer's Italian operation, based in Parma. Arriving in town he found himself—as most people do in Parma, it being the international headquarters of cured-ham consumption—eating and appreciating great prosciutto most every day. This is when Herb underwent the mid-life career change thing. The job switch led him all the way back to Iowa, where he started his work making great prosciutto, guanciale and pancetta. From the beginning he's been focused on using the best hogs he can find, feeding in the old ways and most recently finishing his hogs on acorns. He and his wife, Kathy, use only pork from free-running Iowa hogs and they cure without nitrites (nor do they use the vegetable extracts that most non-nitrite curers employ). In short, Herb's quest for ever-better quality, ever-finer finish and ever-greater complexity is right up our alley.

The La Quercia pancetta starts with Berkshire pork that Herb has cured with black and white peppercorns, juniper, bay leaves and sea salt. His standard cure is currently 60 days—going past that tends to make the meat a bit quicker to smoke in the pan when you cook with it, and since that's how most Americans use pancetta the caution is understandable. But for eating raw the meat grows more tender and richer in flavor with a longer cure. I like it aged up to six months when we can get it that way. Interestingly, when I was eating that pancetta Calabrese, I asked the chef how long it had been aged. "Six to eight months," he answered without hesitating. The man knew his pork, and the fact that it had been aged that long was clearly a point of pride.

Here in the States, Armandino Batali started doing similar things with pancetta about 10 years ago at his tiny shop, Salumi, in downtown Seattle. Like his more famous son Mario, Armandino is almost impossibly nice. He's a retired Boeing engineer, whose story is a combination of Allan Benton's family tradition and Herb Eckhouse's second-career turn. Armandino's maternal grandfather opened the first Italian import food shop in Seattle back in 1903. After three decades as an engineer, Armandino came "back" to the family's food-retailing roots, blending his disciplined attention to process with the craft and emotion of traditional Italian eating. Today, Salumi is run by Armandino's daughter Gina, who spent 20 years as a human resources expert for General Electric, along with her husband, Brian D'Amato.

All the meats they're producing are very good, including the pancetta, of which they make two varieties. One is crafted using pork from a farm just south of the Washington-Oregon border, the other using Berkshire hogs from Newman Farms in Missouri (the same source Sam Edwards buys from). Gina and Brian rub the meat with pepper, salt, spices and a touch of nitrite. Gina is adamant—as are so many others—that the nitrite improves the finished flavor. They hang the bellies for three to four months in order to achieve the same sort of rich tenderness that Herb Eckhouse gets at La Quercia.

Paul Bertolli, previously chef at Chez Panisse and Oliveto in the Bay Area and a producer of very fine traditional Italian salami, has also turned to making pancetta lately. Paul and his crew at his firm, Fra Mani, start by hand-trimming the pork: "All the bellies we'd get in were already skinned, which takes too much fat off," he explained. "So we take in the bellies whole and hand-skin them here and that lets us keep the fat the way we like." The meat is then rubbed with sea salt and celery juice (a natural source of nitrite) and left to set up for three days. It's then re-rubbed with garlic, crushed bay leaf, ground clove and black pepper and aged for about eight days. Although pancetta that's to be eaten raw benefits from a long cure, a short-cured variety like Paul's can still be superb for cooking. Since almost everyone he sells his pancetta to wants to cook with it, he simply opted not to age it out as he would a salami or cured ham that would be eaten uncooked.

Whichever brand you're using, a little bit of good pancetta goes a long way. It's great in pasta carbonara, of course. But you can also use it in vegetable or bean soups, or diced and tossed with cooked clams. Try wrapping fresh figs in slices of pancetta, sticking them with a sprig of fresh rosemary and then running the skewers under the broiler to cook the pork very lightly—I've provided recipes for most of these dishes at the end of the book. John Thorne also shares an excellent recipe in *Simple Cooking* (one of my favorite food books of all time) for pasta with pancetta, celery and white beans: just fry the pancetta, then the celery and finally add the cooked beans.

Or you can do as Paul Bertolli does. "I make a PLT," he told me, as if it were one of the most obvious things in the word. It's a very good sandwich: lightly cooked pancetta, some nice heirloom lettuce and thick slices of the best tomatoes you can get. You can toast an Italian roll and brush it with olive oil (use one that's bold enough to stand up to the pork, but not so big that you overwhelm everything else), or go the more typical American route and make it with mayonnaise. If you're into an exceptionally rich eating experience, try adding slices of burrata, a fresh mozzarella that has been "wrapped" around slivers of more mozzarella and fresh cream.

Lardo

Even our bacon-loving Zingerman's clientele looks askance when we show them a block of pork fat and tell them it costs twenty-something dollars a pound. And that we recommend they eat it raw. But lardo is really delicious, and once one gets over the visuals, it's pretty hard not to be a fan of this Italian-style cured pork fat. Basically, *lardo is to commercial pork fat what a hundred-year-old balsamic vinegar is to a bottle of the supermarket stuff.*

Lardo is a specialty of the tiny hill town of Colonnata, in the still hard-to-reach northeastern corner of Tuscany where Michelangelo used to get his marble. Basically, it's back fat cut from the best-fed, fattest pigs, cured for months with rock salt, rosemary, cloves and "secret" herbs in square marble boxes about two-and-a-half feet a side that are arrayed around marble-walled rooms. The salt pulls the natural liquid out of the pork, producing a brine during the aging process, which both protects and tenderizes the fat. When it's done curing the fat is like butter—an herb butter, I suppose, thanks to those herbs and spices.

Even I reacted with a bit of trepidation the first time someone offered it to me. My first taste came at a remarkable little shop called Giusti, in Modena, a place so small that it makes the original

Zingerman's Deli space look like a superstore. The shop has been there since 1605. In recent times it was run for many years by the late Nano Morandi, and now by his wife and children. We arrived with a small group—I think it was probably about 15 people, which meant the Morandis had to basically close the shop for an hour to squeeze us in. Then they served us a lunch of *aperitivi*: small, wonderful appetizers, the most memorable of which to me was the lardo served alongside freshly fried, pillow-shaped pieces of puffy dough called *gnocco fritto*. You lay a slice of the lardo atop the warm dough and eat it as is. The warmth from the fried gnocco fritto starts a very slight melting of the lardo and . . . I'll leave the rest to your imagination.

Remember that in Europe the fat is the most highly prized part of cured hams like prosciutto. So it only follows that lardo—which basically has no meat to get in the way of the fat—is the ultimate hors d'oeuvre. It's typically served very simply: on gnocco fritto in Modena, or sliced thin, laid atop a slice of warm bread and eaten as is. It's also outstanding on bruschetta: toast some Zingerman's Farm bread, rub it with a cut clove of fresh garlic, pour on a good Tuscan olive oil and top while still warm with slices of lardo. While it's true that you can also use lardo as a seasoning meat the way you would pancetta, eating it raw is really the way to go. It's also great in an old sweet-savory combination on toast with honey (I vote for chestnut honey) and toasted walnuts.

The best I had there was made by Lardera di Colonnata. It's truly amazing. Unfortunately, the producers haven't gone after USDA clearance, so we can't get it here in the States. Fortunately, though, we can now get high-quality versions right here in this country, too, courtesy of the usual suspects: Herb Eckhouse in Iowa, Armandino Batali in Seattle and the Niman Ranch gang based out on the West Coast. All have done a pretty good job of recreating this wonderful Italian specialty. I can't say that any of them have hit me with the same rich butteriness that I think the best Italian versions have, but we'll get there eventually, I'm sure. It just takes time to master this stuff: the Tuscans have had a few thousand years of practice!

Guanciale

From a technical standpoint, guanciale isn't bacon, either. Like lardo, it's made from the wrong part of the pig: in this case, the jowl. But since it's used in a recipe that regularly—if, most Italians will tell you, wrongly—calls for bacon, I figured it would be okay to mention it in passing. It's certainly an interesting bacon alternative.

The name "guanciale" means "pillow" in Italian—a reference to its chewy meatiness and also to the shape of the whole piece of off-white cured jowl. "Cured jowl" probably sounds scary if you haven't tried it, but since this book is directed at bacon lovers let me just say that you'll want to get to know guanciale. Why? Because it's porky, rich, velvety . . . because it's good. It's got pretty much everything most people love about good bacon: perhaps more intensely so, albeit without the smoke. If you need any more convincing, guanciale has been called "the magical Roman bacon." That's a pretty tough label for folks like us to resist.

Personally, I was won over to guanciale thanks to Elizabeth Minchilli, a friend and food writer from St. Louis who has been living in Rome for many years. "I have become a guanciale girl," she says. "I am so much happier cooking with guanciale instead of pancetta." Yow. That got my attention. Forget the Prozac: just switching porks can increase life satisfaction? Who wouldn't want to try it?

"What makes you so high on it?" I asked. "The fat is a different texture, and so takes longer to get to that crunchy stage," she answered. "And when it does, it still remains chewy and has a richer, meatier flavor. I use it for pasta—carbonara, amatriciana—but also with beans," she went on. "I some-

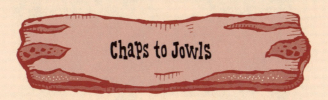

Chaps to Jowls

In Britain, the jowls are referred to as "chaps," a variation on the word "chop." They may also be called Bath Chaps. Either way, it seems that unlike the Italian dry cure for guanciale, chaps are wet brine-cured like the Wiltshire Cut bacon, then rolled in bread crumbs before they're cooked.

times use it in spinach salad, as if it were bacon. This summer I was using it on all sorts of pizza. My favorite was goat cheese, sage and fried guanciale!"

As Elizabeth hinted, guanciale is the most authentic meat to use when you're making pasta all'amatriciana. And there are a handful of very good guanciales on the American market: Niman Ranch cures its fresh hog jowls in sea salt for a month, spices them with rosemary, bay leaf, salt and pepper, and then air-dries them to complete the cure. Herb Eckhouse, too, has been making guanciale for the last few years. "We started making guanciale because we like eating it," he told me. "Next thing we know, we can't keep it in stock." Like Niman's, Herb's is seasoned with salt and spices (most prominently rosemary and black pepper) and then dry-cured. He uses no nitrites, nitrates, vegetable juice or extracts. "The challenge," Herb explained, "is getting the moisture out without making it overly dry." He ultimately settled on a six-week cure, which he feels intensifies the flavor without creating something resembling shoe leather. Up in Seattle, Armandino Batali also makes a very good version. And there are a whole range of good restaurants that are curing their own now, too, perhaps most famously Babbo, the flagship establishment of Armandino's son, Mario.

Bacon Fat,
Pop Music,
Hush Puppies
& Southern
"Olive Oil"

"Dig daddy, it's a natural fact
It's sweepin' the South,
That thing they call the Bacon Fat!"
—Andre Williams, "Bacon Fat"

If you don't like music, food and history you can skip this section altogether. Of course, given the fact that you've read this far, I figure it's probably pretty likely that you like at least the latter two. If not, you'd have long ago tossed this tome onto some dusty stack of abandoned reading materials. And given the high correlation between appreciation for food and love of music, I'm going to guess you'll keep reading. Which is why you're about to embark on the story of an obscure, raunchy, 50-something-year-old song and its relationship to hush puppies and little bowls of hot bacon fat.

I should probably start with the hush puppies. They've been on the menu at the Roadhouse since we opened in the fall of 2003. If you're unfamiliar with them, hush puppies are deep-fried balls of thick cornmeal batter that are served with everything from ketchup to catfish. The story has it that people used to toss bits of cornbread dough to their barking dogs to keep them quiet. True or not they're an epically Southern tradition: one friend of mine who has spent a lot of time in the South told me, "I love hush puppies. They're comforty, they're fried and they taste good and they taste like what you make in big old Southern kitchens."

Hush puppies are already on my mind when our story begins. We'd just added "blue puppies" made from an heirloom blue corn to our standard yellow-corn version (being here in Ann Arbor we couldn't really resist the maize and blue thing—if you don't know what it's about, Google "maize and blue" and you'll find out in about 16 seconds) when a customer who'd grown up in the South stopped me to say that our hush puppies were the best she'd ever eaten. "I just wish my mother were still alive to try them," she enthused.

A few weeks later I headed south for the annual Southern Food-ways Alliance Symposium in Oxford, Mississippi. Traveling in the land where hush puppies were born, I was thinking about how the average hush puppy, while conceptually quite loveable, isn't really all that flavorful. I mean, in the same way that even not very good donuts taste "good" when they're still hot, there's probably something people like about any hush puppy just because it's fried and kind of crunchy on the outside and soft on the inside. But the truth is, like most grits you get served, the average hush puppy is made from flavorless commercial cornmeal, and too often overloaded with ingredients like sugar that are added to mask a lack of corn flavor.

By contrast, our hush puppies start out with exceptionally delicious cornmeal from Anson Mills in South Carolina. Anson Mills raises the old varieties of heirloom corn (low yield, high flavor), field dry it (as opposed to the far faster machine drying) to protect its natural flavors, then stone mill at very low temperatures—downright cold, actually. They leave in the germ, where much of the flavor is, which means that we're working with a full-flavored, fresh, all-natural product that brings way bigger flavor to anything you use it in. Including, of course, your hush puppies. They really taste like corn, not just fried, slightly sweet dough.

The connection—moving from puppies to pork fat—came about courtesy of a very nice couple from South Carolina who stopped in at the Roadhouse one spring evening with their son and his girlfriend, both students at Michigan. The whole family loved their meal, which included a number of Southern and other('n?) things off the menu. The father, a very nice, very down-to-earth guy with a strong South Carolina accent, was particularly complimentary: no small thing for a Southerner to be praising a Northern restaurant's fried chicken, barbecue and grits.

Toward the end of the evening the father gently inquired if I was up for one suggestion on how we could make our food even a little bit better. "Of course!" I answered. "Your hush puppies are really good," he said in a slightly conspiratorial tone. "But you're missing one thing that would really put them over the top." OK, now he had my attention. "Pray tell?" I inquired, anticipating some wisdom from a person who, unlike me, had actually grown up with this stuff. He smiled sort of mischievously, looked me right in the eye, and said, "You need to put a little bacon fat in them."

I thanked him, then thought about it for a minute. "Good idea," I answered. "But"—glancing over at his son, who didn't eat meat— "the vegetarians would kill us!" The son, who I assume had been through this sort of thing with his dad before, didn't say a word. The father shook his head and, smiling broadly, said, "Just don't tell 'em!"

His advice reminded me of how the British Army got into trouble with its Indian Muslim troops in the early twentieth century by using pork fat to grease shell casings. You didn't have to be a historian or even a brilliant businessperson to know that the father's advice wasn't really something you'd want to follow up on. I could imagine the headline: "Zingerman's Sneaks Bacon Fat into Fried Corn." But what I realized the next day was that rather than putting the bacon *in* the puppies, we could just offer guests a small bit of hot bacon fat *on the side*. I mean, it's utterly normal in this country to serve foods with a sauce on the side: French fries come with ketchup, oysters with cocktail sauce, so why not hush puppies with bacon fat? The condiment strategy would allow us to have our vegetarians and eat our bacon fat, too.

Within a few weeks we made it standard procedure for Roadhouse servers to offer up a side of hot bacon fat to any guest who'd ordered hush puppies. Now, a few years later, our regulars ask for it when they place their order. But if I offer it to new customers of non-Southern origin, most still stare back at me with a look somewhere between "That's a joke, right?" and "Are you trying to kill me?"

I explain patiently that bacon fat is the olive oil of the South, that people in that part of the world put bacon fat in, on or next to almost everything they eat, and that bacon fat is actually really good with hush puppies. "It's like eating cornbread with bacon," I often

Bacon Fat Keeps You Fit

Well, that's probably not true, but I was surprised to discover that the nutritional profile of bacon fat really isn't anywhere as bad as most people think it is. I'm not suggesting you should eat endless quantities of the stuff. But if you check the nutritional data, bacon fat actually has only slightly more total fat than butter, and less saturated fat than beef drippings.

Olive oil, by contrast, does have more total fat than bacon, but it's lower in saturated fats and higher in the more desirable monounsaturated type.

add, helping to win a few folks over. "Or think of dipping bread in olive oil. It's really the same thing." While not everyone bites, many do—enough so that that side of hot bacon fat is becoming one of our signature items. In fact, not long ago I got a call from a trade magazine wanting to know what all this bacon fat business at the Roadhouse was about. Bacon, I'm sure you'll soon be reading in the trend-watching food magazines of the world, is the olive oil of North America!

The moment that really put this whole bacon fat business over the top for me came a few weeks later, when I stumbled onto "Bacon Fat" the song. Yes, although hardly anyone today has ever heard of it, back in the fall of 1956—the same year when Mr. Bende's parents were escaping from Hungary—a song by that name, written and recorded by Andre Williams, burst into the national top 10. Never having heard of the man, I immediately looked him up. Turns out he was quite controversial for his overtly sexual lyrics, and innovative for the early talk-over he would do on his records, 25 years or so before rap music was even invented. I soon discovered a whole cadre of loyal Andre Williams fans right in my midst. Skylar Woodman, who worked at the Roadhouse from the time we opened, told me straight off, "I'm a *big* Andre Williams fan." Jim Reische, who edited this book, turned out to be another aficionado. The fact that Williams' catalog included at least a half-dozen food-themed titles like "The Greasy Chicken," "Chicken Thighs," "Do the Popcorn" and "Rib Tips" raised my level of interest still higher. I also learned that the late Lux Interior of The Cramps once described Andre as making Little Richard sound like Pat Boone. And indeed some of his other songs have titles like "Jail Bait," "Loose Juice" and "Sweet Little Pussycat." I'll spare you the lyrics, but you get the idea. Nothing about this situation—the man, the music, the fat—was middle-of-the-road. And, as you know, I like that! I pretty much *needed* to get ahold of this guy's music.

I jumped on the phone, calling every music store in town to try and find a copy of Williams' CD. They all told me they could order it, but I wasn't really in the mood to wait.

The feeling was just like I'd had when I found out about the Wiltshire Cure: my patience went right out the window. I wanted to hear Andre Williams right away. But try as I might, no one in Ann Arbor could get it for me quick enough. So I found a copy online, ordered it and waited (not all that patiently). It was worth it.

"Bacon Fat" would be a hard song to forget even if you weren't really into bacon fat the food. It starts with a low sax solo that makes my head slide from side to side, followed by drums that come up from below, with the backup singers doing a little "wop, wop" thing. Williams waits half a minute or so, humming softly in the background, then gets the lyrics going in that raspy, sly talking style that made him seem so radical at the time. He might never have made the big time, but he did make some great music.

If you'll pardon my less-than-perfect transcription—the lyrics sound way better if you hear them over the actual music, of course—but the song goes kind of like this:

While I was down in Tennessee,
All my friends was glad to see me,
Seein' some down by the railroad tracks,
Seein' some cotton pickers with their sacks on their backs,
They say, "Hey man, we're glad to see you back
We got a new dance it's called the Bacon Fat."

It goes . . . diddly, diddly, diddly

Ohhhhhh . . . have mercy. Hep yo'se'f youngun'
Then you go . . . diddly, diddly, diddly
Oh but the Chicken was never like this.
I feel like I wanna holler, but the town's too small

That's what they say,

Oh . . . but the Chicken was never like this . . .
I feel like I wanna holler,
But the town's too small.
Have mercy!

But then I went down to see my local DJ,
His name is King,
He lived down Tennessee way,

I said, "Hey man, what's this new kind of jump,
Where you wind up twice and then you end up with the bump?"

He said, "Dig daddy, it's a natural fact,
It's sweepin' the South,
That thing they call the Bacon Fat!"

I've listened to "Bacon Fat" a few hundred times by now I'm sure, and I still love it. Every time it comes on the Roadhouse sound system it gets me going! (If you want a visual to accompany the music, you can get a good look at Andre himself in a rather regal pose on the website of his record label, In The Red Records.)

As it turns out, Andre and I share the same approach to work: we love what we do and we plan to keep doing it as long as we can. In a 2008 NPR interview, Williams said, "Do I want to retire? No, no, no. The answer to that is no . . . I do not want to retire. [I'm] just going to keep doing what I do till my body tells me you can't do it no more, Andre. And then I'll produce." After a number of years in the musical wilderness, Andre Williams started making records again in the 1990s, and while his new material is great, raunchy stuff, "Bacon Fat" is still the song that sticks in my head. And on my table.

Crisp or Soft? Do the Bend 'n' Flop

While Andre Williams waxes provocative on the subject of bacon fat, I'm thinking there might be another dance in the making called the "Bend 'n' Flop." The idea comes out of a series of conversations I'd had with various bacon makers about the desirability of various "donenesses." While most every bacon eater has his or her opinion on this issue, I thought I'd go to the source and see what some of the folks who make the bacon have to say. I expected to run into some real differences of opinion, but what I found is that most, if not all, of the producers I spoke to like their bacon on the soft side. Tanya Nueske's answer, was typically decisive: "Definitely softer . . . Definitely. We always try and encourage 'bacon that has some bend.'" Sam Edwards said pretty much the same thing, though the accent shifted from Tanya's northern Wisconsin twang to an eastern Virginia lilt: "I like it a little floppy because if you cook it too long, in my opinion, it gets dried out. I like it fried and cooled down with a little bit of a flop to it." Down at Broadbent's, in southwest Kentucky, the Drennans are what one might call a mixed bacon marriage. "Ronny prefers his bacon almost limp, not real crispy. But I prefer mine crispy," Beth said, sounding a little like she was prepping for an appearance on the Newlywed Game. "I mostly microwave my bacon," she added. "I cook it on a round microwave tray for about four minutes. Usually the bacon on the outside of the tray is crispy and the middle is not quite as done. This is perfect for the two of us. I will fry bacon in a skillet when I'm wanting drippings for other cooking purposes. The drippings aren't nearly as good from the microwave bacon." Allan Benton, though, contributed a more serious entry to the doneness debate. In fact, his response was adamant, and even sort of scientific. "We recommend that people don't overcook it," he said. "We like to take it just until it starts getting crisp. But if you get it too crisp it gets a bit bitter." Allan has tested his bacon pretty extensively over the years, so I'm going to take his word on this.

In thinking about the subject over the ensuing months it dawned on me that the bias toward softer bacon makes perfect sense. I have a theory that people like me who are inclined to the crispy side developed our preference by eating commercial bacon earlier in life. Because the flavor of the actual pork in those mass-market products is relatively low, the crispness and slight charring overrides the lack of flavor. It's like drinking cheap beer very cold. Feels refreshing, but it's more about the mouthfeel and the cooling effect than about any kind of complexity.

Of course, while the experts have their preference for the softer side, you and I can eat our bacon any way we want. But you may find it interesting to taste-test the same brand of bacon at two or three different degrees of doneness.

Jews and Bacon

Well, here's a strange and rather taboo-ish topic. But hey, let's break down the barriers and check it out.

One reason that I think olive oil and bacon are parallel for me is because both were so alien to my upbringing. As I've mentioned, bacon was an all-out taboo. And, although olive oil could certainly have been served in a kosher kitchen, in practice it was almost entirely absent from any part of my childhood, other than reading about it in the Bible or hearing the story of the miracle of Chanukah. I don't think anyone had anything against it. It just wasn't a big part of the Eastern European Jewish or mid-twentieth-century Midwest eating experiences.

From a broader cultural perspective, I find it odd how many jokes Jewish people who don't keep kosher make about bacon. Somehow, bacon seems to be embedded in our Jewish brains. It's the forbidden fruit: the thing you want specifically because you're not supposed to. Bill Niman, who started Niman Ranch and is a nice Jewish boy from Minneapolis, laughed out loud when I asked him about this subject. "Most Jewish people don't consider bacon *treyf* (forbidden food), do they? It's more like a species of its own."

When it comes to Jewish bacon consumption, you really won't see the multi-generation histories that characterize so much of the production end I've been telling you about. But there is a legacy of sorts. For example, it was a Jewish PR man—Freud's nephew, Edward Bernays—who began the transformation of bacon and eggs into the all-American breakfast. And Biblical bacon bans aside, it turns out there are a LOT of Jewish folks processing pork around the U.S. Take Herb Eckhouse in Iowa, or Nathan Marcus, who's got a big project going in Kentucky to make traditional Italian porchetta (high-heat pork roast in the style of central Italy) from heirloom-breed hogs. Or Bruce Aidells. Elizabeth Minchilli, the Guanciale Girl, is actually a nice Jewish girl from St. Louis. And there's Joeli Yaguda's Jewish (but she can eat a pound of bacon) olive oil-making mother-in-law, Karen Guth. Even my bacon-loving editor, Jim Reische, who told me that his mother "still feels revulsion at the thought of pork." Clearly, the list is a long one.

The challenge is probably particularly interesting in the South, where bacon and pork fat play such a prominent role in people's everyday eating. It's not easy to avoid the stuff unless you dine in every night. Morrie Lipton, a retired surgeon from South Carolina who grew up keeping kosher in the South and still does today, told me "They have all these great vegetables. But 80 percent of them are cooked with bacon. So we couldn't eat them." Marcie Ferris, who's done a lot of research and writing on Southern Jewish cooking, told me that "Most of the stories I've heard concerning southern Jews and bacon are usually about quirky southern rules of *Kashrut* [kosher law]. Like, 'My mother didn't eat bacon on Shabbos.'"

Most everywhere I travel in the food world, people tip me off to another Jewish chef I should talk to about pork. I'm pretty sure this is a graduate thesis waiting to be written. I'm not sure what it says about Jewish culture, the spirit of rebellion or the work of Sigmund Freud, but it sure is funny in an interesting way.

To top it all off, about 10 days before I finished this manuscript I discovered that Andre Williams, the man who brought us "Bacon Fat," converted to Judaism! While I don't get the sense that the Orthodox rabbinate is ready to recognize his conversion, the coincidence is certainly strange enough. Will bacon wonders never cease?

Vegetarians, Bacon and the Baco-tarians

As often as I've heard about the phenomenon over the years, I continue to be surprised by the number of former vegetarians I find who have a strong attraction to bacon. I'm not joking: I think I meet (or meat?) at least one or two a week.

Gauri Thergaonkar, who worked for us at Zingerman's for many years, grew up in India, where half the population is vegetarian and another 10 percent or so are Muslims who shun pork. As a member of the former group, Gauri ate no meat for the first 32 years of her life. "But," she told me, "I owe bacon a big debt. Bacon was what made me not be vegetarian any more." "I think the bacon thing really started when I was in Washington, DC, at a friend's place," she said. "We were cooking an Indian dinner for a bunch of his friends. Him, having *vindaloo* (made with pork). I was having *paneer* (cheese). We started with the standard American curry base—garlic, ginger, onions and spices. Then he put some bacon in his and I put tomatoes in mine . . . So a few weeks later I'm cooking dinner. I take a deep whiff to decide what to put in next and what should pop into my mind? Bacon. It blew me away. I'd never cooked bacon before . . . Never. I decided right then that I was too serious about food to remain a vegetarian . . . And now, here I am. A firm believer that everything is better with bacon."

When I took this one step further and thought about what it would be like to be a Jewish vegetarian, the challenge seemed almost overwhelming. Brooke Keesling, animator and director of the award-winning short film "Boobie Girl," actually lived it. "To me," she said, "bacon = pure goodness. For the approximately 10 years that I was a vegetarian, the smell of bacon cooking never lost its appeal." Brooke's back to eating meat now and bacon is still, she says, at the top of her list.

Then you have what I've come to call the baco-tarians, a whole class of people who don't consume any meat other than bacon. There are more of them around than you'd think. I wonder if they should have their own special cabins at Camp Bacon . . .

Remember That Top Ten List?

10. The Tree Connection

So . . . back to the bacon tree from page 38, which you've probably forgotten about, unless you flipped ahead. What's the connection?

The story goes like this: back in the eighteenth century somewhere out west a group of American cavalry soldiers were lost in the wilderness. They were starving, no food for days. As they approached a small hill they happened on an old Jewish man resting in the shade. Barely able to walk, the soldiers straggled up to him and asked, desperately, if he knew where they could find something to eat. "Vell," he said, "I hoyd there vas a bacon tree up on the other side of the hill. But I'm not supposed to send you there." The soldiers got excited. A bacon tree? Just over the hill? What could be better? Despite the old man's warnings they set off over the hill, where they were immediately attacked by a group of bandits. All the soldiers were killed except for the captain, who crawled back to where the old man was sitting. "Oy vey, vat happened?" the old man asked. The captain gasped out his story. "Why didn't you warn us?" he wailed. "Vait a minute," said the Jewish fellow. He reached into his pocket, pulled out his Yiddish-English dictionary and started flipping through the pages. Suddenly he stopped and slapped his head. "Oy!" he said, "I feel terrible! It vasn't a 'bacon tree.' It vaz a 'ham-bush!'"

OK, now go make one of these bacon-based dishes for dinner!

The Little Blue Book:
Mao, Maynard, Bacon Curing &
a Modern-Day Cultural Revolution

It's become increasingly clear to me as I work, learn and write about the diverse influences of the bacon world that there are dozens of dots to be connected, many links to be made between people and places, all sorts of strange tie ins to various times in history, that . . . well, cross connections that normaler (sic) people would never see, but that I like, and that I think make the lives of everyone involved more rewarding. So, as we head toward the final stages of this book, I want to move us forward from the racy rock 'n' roll of the 1950s on to bacon curing and life lessons from late-twentieth-century Britain. But just to make matters really interesting I'm going to take us down a bit of a socio-cultural side road, traveling to the UK by way of China and the writings of Chairman Mao.

You read that right; we're going from "Bacon Fat" over to Britain, but we're taking a Long March to make the trip. Although I've only mentioned Mao in reference to his love for the bacon-based dish known as hongshao rou, he's clearly far better-known in the world at large for the Chinese Revolution. I've no interest in advocating for his politics here, but I am a history major and he was a larger-than-life figure long before I found out he was a big bacon-eater. Back in the 1960s, Mao's *Little Red Book* became one of the best-selling essays ever put into print. In the peak years of its popularity during the 1960s and '70s, some five- or six-million copies of the handbook for the Cultural Revolution were printed. In it, Mao offered up bits of information, ideas and social theory, all meant to outline the way life would be lived in a properly organized and operated society. A lot of it was, of course, driven by Communist Party ideology and is long since out of date. But some of what he said still resonates today—"It is necessary," he wrote, "to investigate both the facts and the history of a problem in order to study and understand it"—a statement that certainly rings true for me, and is really the basis of everything behind this little book on bacon.

In fact, it's that very "investigation of fact and history" that led me to read Maynard's *Adventures of a Bacon Curer* in the first place. And although I'm guessing that their politics are worlds apart, I somehow managed to see Mao and Maynard standing side by side in my mind. At first I thought the connection was way too silly to be mentioned in public. But hey, we've come this far together, so stay with my madness for a minute and I'll explain the connection.

For starters, my mind got going just because of their alliterative, one-word names—Mao and Maynard—was just too good a match to miss out on! More meaningfully, I got to thinking about what Mao and his *Little Red Book* meant to Chinese history. And from red my mind moved to blue and . . . well, as you'll recall, that's the color of the cover of Maynard's book.

Now, mind you, the cover of *Adventures of a Bacon Curer* is nothing one would write home (or probably anywhere else) about. It's as likely to win an award from one of those fancy art magazines as the retail space at Benton's Country Ham is to show up in a center spread for *Architectural Design*. I still chuckle every time I look at it. The cover is just . . . well, it's very . . . *blue*. Now, that's not a bad thing, to be blue. But his cover is about seven different shades of blue. And not particularly appealing shades, either. If you look at a lot of books (and I do, as you may have guessed) his is that kind of stereotypically low-cost cover work that you might see from a small publisher doing a low-budget run of a title they like, but don't expect to sell in very large quantities.

In its own way though, the cover's low-budget oddness probably contributes to the cult and kitsch that seem to have surrounded the book in Britain back when it came out. (It was called Britain's "cult book of the year" back in 2003.) It's what I think designers call two-color art, printed on a kind of low-cost, glossy cardboard cover. The blues range from a faded powder blue (that I suppose you might optimistically say looks a bit like the old Wedgwood pottery, or like what William Johnson back in North Carolina would call "Tarheel blue") on up to something resembling the dark, *bleu de travail* coveralls that European workmen often wear. Add in a bit of white and you've got the whole color scheme in a nutshell.

So when you pick up the book, you find yourself looking at a photo of Maynard, the main man of British bacon, shown in living blue (not black) and white rubbing down a piece of raw pork on an old wooden (again, blue) curing table. That sounds moderately normal enough, I suppose. But the thing is, he's got this big smile and a (I say this respectfully) kind of crazy, wild-eyed look on him, bushy hair and big framed black glasses, with a striped (blue, of course) butcher's apron. I have to confess that the photo makes me think about Peter Sellers, or maybe a Monty Python spoof, definitely not about a serious food scholar or a star chef. Going on looks alone, you'd have to put him a lot closer to a work-ingman's Tom Jones singing on

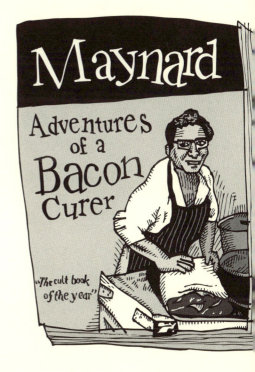

Saturday night in some pub in Portsmouth, than the more glamorous image that his affinity to single-name kindred like Madonna or Prince might otherwise imply.

But while Maynard's tone is light, his work is meaningful in a way that I think moves him more toward Mao, back to a utopian world in which bacon tasted better and people were more trustworthy. Which is how, in the circuitous way that my mind works, I came around to thinking of *Adventures of a Bacon Curer* as "The Little Blue Book"—something we could all gain from carrying around, an accessible and down-to-earth, easy-to-read reference for working through life in a positive and upstanding way, but all centered around great-tasting traditionally made food—primarily, of course, bacon. Maynard's demeanor is far more modest than Chairman Mao's. But in its own way, his message is just as meaningful and revolutionary.

The more I thought about how Maynard's good work could guide us all—bacon lovers or not—toward a better future, the more the image stuck in my head. I don't think the book will ever sell millions of copies but I like the idea of thousands of members of the Slow Food Nation (see slowfoodnation.org for more on the subject) following Maynard down some main street, holding a copy of his tome in hand the way Mao was waving the *Little Red Book* in all those old illustrations done in China circa 1977. Maybe Maynard's long march would work to get ever more people to move back toward good bacon, and in the process to improve the quality of their lives at every level.

The funny thing is that as much as the cover captivated me, it actually almost put me off from one of the best reads I've had in a long time; its unstylish nature could easily lead you to write the book off as some sort of bad 1970s food spoof. Which would be a big mistake: I'll tell you now that I think it's a very good book. I had to page through it multiple times to get at everything in it, not because it's hard to read, but because it's layered with a lot of low-flash wisdom and insight about bacon and life that are easy to miss if you're not paying attention.

There's a bit of personal memory there too, I guess, in my focus on the cover art. My mother passed away in spring 2008, 42 years to the day after Mao declared the launch of the Cultural Revolution. And Maynard's book makes me think about those seemingly silly things that we all pick up from our parents when we're young. You know, those throwaway phrases that, almost unconsciously, stay with you. While I'm pretty sure that my mother never ever ate bacon in her entire kosher-keeping life (and maybe it's for the best that she didn't have to live to see an errant son write a whole tome about it), she did always tell me that, "you can't judge a book by its cover." It's hardly a phrase she coined herself, but for whatever reason she used to say it a lot and it's still the sound of her voice that comes up whenever I hear it in my head. While I can't say that my mother was always right, her words were ridiculously accurate in regards to *Adventures of a Bacon Curer.*

(Speaking of slightly strange, I was reading the sequel to the little blue book—entitled *Secrets of a Bacon Curer*—well after I'd written this whole bit about covers. In it, Maynard tells the story of going out to buy a new car. Although he was ready to buy a nice one, the salesman writes him off immediately because of his farmwear. Maynard makes his original intentions known, but decides to make his purchase elsewhere because of the way he's been treated. After politely but firmly setting the salesman straight, he says, "I knew by his tone he was defeated. He really had made a mistake and the old saying, 'You should not judge a book by its cover' rings true on this occasion." Coincidence? Draw your own conclusions.)

All that said, by the standards of the straight publishing world, I'm not sure how much sense it makes for me to devote half a dozen pages of my own book on bacon to talk about just the cover of another book on bacon. But I've devoted much of my working life to stuff that most everyone says you're not supposed to do, so . . . I'm going to put this part in here regardless of what others might deem to be "appropriate." In my gut, it seems a fitting way to move toward the end of this tome because, really *Adventures of a Bacon Curer* taught me as much about life as it did about bacon. And really so much of my work for the last 30 years has been helping to take "fancy" food out of the mode of some trendy, frou-frou fad to show that it's really all about traditional, down-to-earth eating that's tied to culture, history, ethnography, economics, religion, ritual and right thinking. And, in its own loveable meandering way, that's what Maynard's little blue book is all about, too.

Once you move past the cover, you'll find that although the title credits only "Maynard," the author's last name is actually no secret. It's Davies, and I'm not sure exactly why the publisher chose to use just the first name. If you skim the work too quickly (as I did, the first time through) you'll also probably miss the publisher's note on page vi which lets you know that the book was actually "written" by Maynard's wife, Ann, who transcribed it all from tape recordings. Maynard himself is severely dyslexic, and really can't read or write. In hindsight, knowing that helped me understand why the book comes across as so conversational, roughish and a bit unpolished (but in a good way). Regardless of who hit the actual keys, the man's voice comes through with flying colors.

The great thing, to me, about the Little Blue Book (and its sequel) is that the whole work—while literally about bacon—is actually as much about how Mr. Davies works past his disability and ends up living his life in a positive setting of learning, love, happiness, family and, of course, very good cured pork! I've read it through three times, and the more I go back to it the more I like it. It's got a lot of pretty profound stuff in it, all put down on paper in Maynard's gentle but opinionated and very well-grounded way. It's meaty, it's meaningful and often very moving; although the cover looks loopy, the text made me tear up numerous times.

Leaving behind my Red Book/Blue Book analogy, Maynard's work is probably more fittingly paired philosophically with less political, more spiritually oriented authors. I guess you could say he's kind of like a Kahlil Gibran of pork curing, liberally interspersing wisdom with bacon recipes and curing techniques. "The secret of life," he shares at one point, "is seizing as much happiness when you can. If you leave it too long, and look for happiness later, it may be too late, so the secret is, when the happiness is there, take it and we did." If you take the time to read it, this really is sort of a "better living through bacon" kind of book. No sex, no drugs, no late-night wine-drinking binges—it's really not good material at all for Anthony Bourdain, but I like it a lot.

I don't know that the image has merit any place other than in the strangeness of my own mind, but I also keep thinking of Maynard as a calm, but compelling, sort of Don Quixote, passing through the food world fighting against meanness of spirit, uncaring methods of modernization (what he calls "speed and greed" factories), corporate takeovers and the commensurate smashing of old artisan-oriented machinery, a host of British bureaucrats and of course, bad bacon. En route he advocates for a caring and gentle approach to everything he encounters. He takes time to appreciate the little things, consistently shows a sincere spirit of generosity and supports sustainable farming and fair pricing (as in the type where the producer charges a reasonable price so he can stay in business).

In *The Little Red Book*, Mao wrote that "Whoever wants to know a thing has no way of doing so except by coming into contact with it, that is, by living (practicing) in its environment . . . If you want knowledge, you must take part in the practice of changing reality. If you want to know the taste of a pear, you must change the pear by eating it yourself . . . If you want to know the theory and methods of revolution, you must take part in revolution. All genuine knowledge originates in direct experience." Which, shifting from "red" to "blue," is a pretty remarkably accurate assessment of what Maynard has done with bacon—he's lived it from the time he was a teenager, and by curing it, cooking it and living his life with it, he's made his bacon and the lives of the people who come into contact with it better for the eating. In his case, the "revolution," (which, given the popularity of the Food Network, actually could end up being televised), is about a return to making better bacon and treating everything around him respectfully in the process. The truth is that in the American sense of John Wayne-style winning, Maynard is not a huge hero. But in the context of old-time curing, of storytelling, of learning and of imparting life lessons that benefit bacon, hogs, and humans alike, the man is a winner all the way.

Adventures of a Bacon Curer starts out with Maynard's teenage decision to leave school and look for a job. After a failed apprenticeship with an auto mechanic who judges him by his dyslexia, he gets sent to work with an old-school bacon curer. The rest of the story follows Maynard's bacon-curing capers, starting with his artisan bacon-making mentor, on through to travels to the U.S., where he stays with an Amish family and works in a prison, before returning to the English countryside to manage a small farm where he can go back to the old ways of curing.

The American Amish visit is particularly interesting to me. The recipe he learns while there dates to the 1820s, and, as was true of so much of Colonial-era cooking, actually originated in Maynard's native England. The written recipe was stored safely folded up in the Amish family's Bible for decades. Their grandmother, who shared it with him, talks of traveling cross-country—heading all the way from the coast to central Pennsylvania was a long journey back then, and, bacon was, of course, one of the traveler's staple foods. The recipe is basically a wet cure of water with what Maynard calls "black sugar," which I think is an English name for a very dark, strongly flavored, molasses-left-in, brown sugar.

Throughout the book Maynard mentions at least 20 different bacon cures: there are recipes for pork cured with everything from black treacle to coriander to honey, some dry and some wet cures, most smoked. His bias, if you're wondering, is toward English oak and maybe applewood. The old dry-cured bacons are almost unknown in England today, but hopefully with Maynard's leadership some will be restored to their rightful place at the top of the bacon world—Melvin Ling is doing his part at Appleyards (see page 99). At the end of the book Maynard and wife sell their farm and move on to the next chapter of their life. The sequel, *Secrets of a Bacon Curer,* continues his story from there. Hilariously—to me at least, but I'm strange—the cover features exactly the same photo as the first book, but this time done up in brown!

One of the best things about the *Bacon Curer* books is that Maynard so beautifully captures the essence of finding a vocation. Unlike the more common approach to work ("TGIF" and all that), a vocation is when we work at something that makes us feel truly fulfilled, and which we go at with great passion every day. And we do it, not for short-term material benefit, but because we feel positively wedded to the work, at peace with the processes at play and fulfilled for following them through to fruition. It's honestly the way I feel about my own work, and I count myself incredibly fortunate to be in that spot. I know I'm not the only one—I've talked to plenty of people for whom I've got enormous respect who've shared similar stories.

As you've probably realized from reading about them, many of the folks who make the artisan bacons clearly fall into this category. Allan Benton, Tanya Nueske, Sam Edwards and most of the others are all pretty darned passionate about what they do. There are far easier ways to make a living than crafting old-style bacons, but these folks love their work and it shows in the quality of what they cure. I feel fortunate to know them as people and to experience their products. I think we'd all be standing right behind Mr. Davies should he take the lead on a food-focused Long March. And I don't think any of us would argue with the sentiment he shares when he says, "I belonged to an era where the customer comes first and the quality of the product comes first and the people who taught me my trade were good-hearted and their attitude was the most important thing. I was going to live by that and I felt I owed it to all the people who had taught me curing, including the Quakers in America who had shown me their way of life. I wanted to carry on their traditions, so my principle has always been: 'good food for good people.'"

I'm there with him all the way; it's really what my work is all about. Like Mr. Davies and all these other bacon makers, I'm pretty devoted to the work of the world of good food; I love learning about it and it's incredibly rewarding to teach, taste and share what I know with others who are equally interested. Which is, I guess, what a vocation is all about.

I'm hardly the world's expert on why some people find a "calling" while others just have a "career," and still others are barely able to wait for the weekend. And I've yet to see anyone put down a definitive theory on how to make a calling come to be. I have my own ideas on the subject, but we'll save those for another book. In the moment, suffice it to say, I think there are many ways for each of us to increase the odds of getting there, and Maynard's Little Blue Book certainly leads us in the right direction. While I've plowed through plenty of high-powered (and very good) writings on the subject, Maynard sums up the whole thing in a couple of quiet sentences. "Curing," he shares, "is the kind of job in which you never know it all because every curing session is different. I'm not talking about modern bacon, I'm talking about applying your skill with the best materials to produce something exactly right, so that a customer can sit down and say, 'That's the best piece of bacon I have ever eaten.'"

A Closing Note on the Cost of Better Bacon

Speaking of the best bacon, before we wrap this all up I should come back to some of the basics of buying. This bit really can be pretty quick, but it's worth stating: No matter how you slice it (sorry), *better bacon is pretty much always going to cost a lot more per pound than the mediocre alternative.* I doubt that's going to come as a shock to anyone who has read this far. At the end of the economic day, it simply costs more to raise better hogs, feed them a better diet, slaughter them more humanely, process their pork more carefully and do the smoking and curing correctly. All this while foregoing shortcuts like raising livestock in confinement, or pumping up their meat with water and phosphates. For me, and I'd guess for you, it's well worth the added cost to eat a food whose flavor is so much better, and that's imbued with the history of its making, as with each of the bacons I've written about here.

That said, you and I often need to make the case to others we work, shop or eat with. I've been making it for many years now. But I was struck by the way that Maynard Davies did so in *Adventures of a Bacon Curer*, and I thought I'd share just one more piece of his gentle wisdom with you. "There is an old saying in our business," he writes. "'The price is forgotten but the taste is remembered.'" Now that, I think, is a simple and totally true way to sum it up. "I had one or two customers," he continues, "who always asked how much (the bacon) would cost and I used to tell them, then the moment of truth would come when they decided whether they wanted it or didn't. But the people who really looked after themselves, and invested in themselves, never bothered about the price: all they wanted was good food to eat."

The End:
Heading Home from Camp

Anyone who's been away to camp probably knows that bittersweet feeling that sets in when the season comes to an end: happy to be heading back to more familiar surroundings, yet, at the same time, sad to see the summer go. A hundred good memories saved up: a few fade quickly, while others linger pleasantly for the rest of our lives. I figure that's kind of how things would feel at Camp Bacon: a certain sense of achievement for having finished the book (and from me, genuine appreciation for your having stuck with it), a sense of smoky sadness as we get down to the last few pages. Leaving it all behind . . . for a while, at least. All of which made me think of fitting ways to bring the book, and Camp Bacon, to a worthy and worthwhile conclusion.

At the Ann Arbor Folk Festival each year, the evening ends with all of the show's performers coming back out on stage to sing a song or two together. Because the musicians come from all over the country, you get this great diversity in style of dress, age, voice and cultural origin. You often wind up with 25 or 30 people on stage together, performing as a group for the first time. Each year's show is unique—the song and the spirit of that finale are always different because the performers are different from one year to the next. Yet, somehow, it works. The whole thing comes together because the stage is filled with people who care deeply about their music, who love writing, playing and performing, and who have made this the focus of their life's work.

One afternoon I had this image that when Camp Bacon came to a close for the year, I wanted to borrow the Folk Festival model and create a comparable wrap-up for all the people who've played such a big part in the world of cured pork. I know it's a little odd, but I had this image of bringing all the centuries of great bacon "players" I've been writing about up on stage together.

I'd start by introducing the modern-day bacon makers: Sam Edwards, Tanya Nueske and Allan Benton. I'd have to add in Nancy Newsom, whose country ham I love: although she doesn't make her own bacon, she does sell Charlie Gatton's and I've always referred to her as the "Lucinda Williams of country ham," so she should definitely be up there. Charlie Gatton himself, as well—his name makes him sound like someone who plays country music as well as curing country bacon. Herb Eckhouse, the nation's leading Jewish bacon curer, would have to be there, along with those Italian-American pancetta producers, the Batali family and Paul Bertolli. Bring in Bruce Aidells, another nice Jewish boy, to sing some bass. Add Irishmen like Tommy Maloney and Englishmen like the two Williams—

Tullberg and Johnson (who by now must be an honorary Brit). The Canadian Ken Haviland is there to help out. And Mr. Bende, of course, with his doubly smoky, quiet Hungarian-accented voice in the background.

Moving out of the modern era, we'd call up Harrison Ainsworth, author of *The Flitch of Bacon*, along with the Dunmow prior who came up with the idea of "bringing home the bacon" in the twelfth century. I'd whistle on a conch shell to summon the original drovers, William and John Pynchon from Massachusetts (who surely sang or whistled while they walked their hogs). We'd not want to leave out the modern-day band The Drovers, who bear the name of the Pynchons' long-since-disappeared profession. And we'd have to have the Harris family over from Wiltshire to add a traditional British touch to our tunes.

Of course we'd have a big stage to fill, so why stop there? There are writers to be accounted for: Harriette Arnow for sure, because she's one of my heroes and because she wrote so beautifully about a way of life in the Kentucky and Tennessee hills that had so much influence on the way we cure and cook bacon today. George Lang without question—he actually played the violin, so he'd be quite an asset. Can't forget Maynard Davies, the main man of modern British bacon curing, nor the original Guanciale Girl, Elizabeth Minchilli. Edward Bernays would be backstage, of course, scripting a well-orchestrated finale with his Uncle Sigmund. And speaking of uncles, I definitely would want the Zingerman's-connected bluegrass-playing women from Uncle Earl up there doing "Streak o' Lean, Streak o' Fat." Mao, as well, a dish of hongshao rou in one hand, copies of both the Little Blue and Little Red books in the other. While he's merely a recipe footnote in this book (see page 158), how could you *not* have Johnny Cash up there singing and playing guitar while eating one of his burgers topped with Folsom Prison sauce? Speaking of being so bad you're good (or is it, so good, you're bad?), I definitely want to get Sarah Katherine Lewis up there to add passion and the sort of out-of-the-mainstream mindset and (bacon-) magic I'm so drawn to. And, of course, last but the opposite of least, we'd absolutely for sure want Andre Williams out front working the crowd.

The funny thing is, for a minute I actually couldn't figure out what song this illustrious, cross-cultural group of baconeers should sing. But then, fortunately, my brain reengaged, and I realized the incredibly obvious, which is that they'd pretty much *have* to perform "Bacon Fat." Andre would take the lead, and everyone else would be singing along, dancing and doing backup vocals, as needed. Now that's a scene I can come to terms with. A thousand years of bacon curing, culture and cooking all combined into one seriously smoky, rich, memorably meaty end-of-the-season, musical composition.

Endings for me are sad. I'm glad to head home, but it's still hard to leave where I've been. The good news is that in this case you can bring a little bit of Camp Bacon back with you to your kitchen. If you add up what you've learned while you were "here," the recipes in the following pages and the creative thoughts that I'm confident will have come up from within, I'm guessing you'll have plenty of good bacon activity to keep you busy for years to come.

Coming back to our learning objectives from the beginning of the book, we had four, and I figure we should check to see if we've actually achieved them.

It's probably safe to say that if you've made it this far you've successfully achieved goal #1: to learn more about bacon and its history than you'd ever imagined you'd be interested in.

As for #2: take the Trivia Test on page 221. I'm rooting for you. In terms of knowing your favorite bacons and what you want to do with them: go to it!

On, then, to objective #3: know your favorite bacon. Most likely you'll have to eat, not just read, to make that happen. But if you've got access to better bacon (and there's always mail order!), I have to hope that you're well on your way to making this one a reality as well.

And finally there's #4: being ready to go home and make the recipes in the book. I hope you're hungry. Please know that I'd be happy to help you, or direct you to friends who know more than

I do. You can email me at baconbits@zingermans.com if you have cooking questions and I'll do my best to assist.

So there you go: the end of the season at Camp Bacon. While bacon has certainly been at the top of the culinary hit parade over the last few years, it's the lasting culinary contribution that bacon has made (and is still making) to our culture and our cooking that has drawn me to it. I hope you feel the same way.

Last word here goes to the late chef and food writer Bill Neal. This quote, from his book *Southern Cooking*, helps me imagine a really good last-night meal at Camp Bacon. It's something our happy band of onstage baconeers could happily have gathered to eat at a post-show party. I know it makes me hungry—and happy— every time I read it.

> *Bacon frying is almost always irresistible. In a mountain forest, by a limpid stream, at sunset, over an open fire, it beckons more seductively than Circe. When coupled with the rewards of an honest fisherman—fresh trout fried till crisp, ash-roasted baby potatoes, and, in the spring, perhaps a handful of freshly chopped ramps tossed into the sputtering fat—it creates my ideal of a great meal: strong, fresh flavors in equal combat, food that sustains, not just entertains.*

Keep on fryin'! See you next season!

Ari

Recipes

42 WAYS TO PUT BACON TO WORK IN YOUR KITCHEN

Recipe Index

As Sam Keen wrote in *Hymns to an Unknown God,* "You can starve to death trying to eat a cookbook." So now that you've worked your way through all those words about bacon, it's time to start cooking! One of the challenges when I write recipes is that I'm what Maggie Bayless (managing partner at ZingTrain) refers to as "unconsciously competent." That is, I've become so used to doing things a certain way that I forget to share some very important information. In order to help you achieve the same level of enjoyment these recipes have brought to me, I figured I should start this section with a quick note about some of the basics.

I've already alluded to the importance of great ingredients. And I'll do so any number of more times in the recipes that follow. As anyone who cooks a lot knows well already, the little things really do make a big difference. But this is a point worth emphasizing. Start with the best ingredients you can buy: olive oil, for me, always means extra virgin (and there are wide variations in quality even then); vinegars are naturally converted and well-aged; parmesan is Parmigiano-Reggiano; salt is sea salt; and black pepper is Tellicherry. (For more details on these and other interesting ingredients, pick up a copy of *Zingerman's Guide to Good Eating.*)

This is all especially important here because many of the bacon recipes are so simple. Mac and Grease made with mediocre pasta and bad bacon instead of Martelli and well-cured pork is likely to be . . . not very tasty. Mush and Bacon made with standard commercial cornmeal might be warm and filling, but won't even remotely approach the culinary awakening I attained when making it with Anson Mills' meal for the first time. Humble celery, a vegetable that most people take for granted, has lately become one of my passions: the difference between the commercial stuff most of us grew up on and the intense and delicious flavor that you get from locally grown heirloom celery is as radical as the difference between bad super-market bacon and Allan Benton's best.

Speaking of bacon, in these recipes you'll find bacon measured out both in weight and number of slices. Roughly speaking, a slice is 1½ to 2 ounces of pork. The challenge is, of course, that since this stuff isn't being extruded out of some high-tech machine controlled by laser beams, each slice of artisan bacon is unique. Not to mention that different brands and cures will render different amounts of fat. Ultimately, each recipe designates the amount of bacon I happen to like. You can—and should—adjust up or down to fit your own taste, mood, time of year or astrological sign. So, long story short, the quantities listed in these recipes offer a good way to start, but once you get the hang of it go with your gut: cook, taste, adjust and then do it all again!

If you have questions or uncertainties—if I can help you find ingredients or assist you with your cooking—by all means, drop me an email any time. It's baconbits@zingermans.com.

Happy cooking! And don't forget the bacon fat!

Bacon Hash

This hash has turned out to be a hit with most everyone who's had it. It's an excellent way to take advantage of the big flavor of top-of-the-line bacons. The bacon is the headliner rather than just a couple of strips alongside another main dish. I like making it with the dry-cured intensity of the Broadbent's, Benton's, Father's or Edwards', but it really would work with any good bacon.

You can make the recipe a day or two in advance if you like, then reheat it in a skillet when you're ready to serve. Regardless, you'll want to cook both the bacon and potatoes and let them cool before you move on to the rest of the recipe.

Serve with rye toast and a couple of poached eggs if you like, as well.

Ingredients:

4 tablespoons rendered bacon fat
1 medium onion, coarsely chopped
1 medium red bell pepper, coarsely chopped
1 stalk celery, coarsely chopped
2 tablespoons flour
1½ cups chicken broth
2 teaspoons Worcestershire sauce
10 ounces sliced bacon (about 5 to 7 slices), lightly cooked and chopped
2 pounds potatoes (I like Yukon Golds, German Butterballs or others of that
     ilk), steamed over salted water until tender, then diced with the skins on
¼ cup heavy cream
Coarse sea salt to taste
Freshly ground Tellicherry black pepper to taste

Procedure:

Melt the bacon fat in a large skillet over moderate heat. Add the onion, bell pepper and celery and cook, covered, for 5 to 6 minutes, until soft.

Sprinkle the flour over the wilted vegetables and stir well to avoid lumps. Cook for another 4 to 5 minutes, stirring constantly to keep from sticking, until the flour blends with the bacon fat into a thickened roux.

Add the broth, a bit at a time, stirring well after each addition so the mixture stays smooth and creamy. The sauce should coat the back of your spoon before you add more liquid. Stir in the Worcestershire sauce.

Continue simmering the sauce over moderate heat until it thickens, about 5 minutes. Add the bacon and potatoes and mix well. Add the cream and cook, stirring, a few more minutes. Stir in salt and freshly ground pepper to taste.

Serve immediately, or cool and reheat in a skillet until you get a nice golden brown crust.

Serves 4 to 6 as a main dish

Hangtown Fry

Oysters, eggs and bacon in one really good all-American dish, Hangtown Fry is a California classic that's long been one of the most popular items on the Roadhouse brunch menu. I love it because it's simple to make, it's delicious and it's got a great story to boot. I like to use a dry-cured bacon like Broadbent's because that's the sort of intense, long-cured bacon that Gold Rush-era cooks would likely have been working with.

The story of Hangtown Fry takes you to a northern California town originally known as Old Dry Diggins, then as Hangtown and now Placerville. Back in Gold Rush days it was a prominent supply town—many of the area's miners went there to restock and cut loose, and, while they were at it, often got themselves into a bit of trouble. The name Hangtown came about in the middle of the nineteenth century, when three bad guys were strung up on the branches of a big old oak in the center of town. I've been told that the stump of that old oak is still "stuck in the mud" (so to speak) in the basement of a bar called The Hangman's Tree (which you'll be able to find quickly by the body hanging from a noose off the front of the building).

For whatever reasons, the area seems to have a good bit of both baconic and creative criminal energy emanating from it. About 40 miles east and slightly north of Sacramento, Hangtown isn't far from the better-known town of Folsom. Folsom was made musically famous by Johnny Cash's "Folsom Prison Blues" in 1956, which seems to have been something of a banner year for bacon—in a 12-month period Andre Williams released the single of "Bacon Fat," Mr. Bende and his people fled west out of Hungary from the Revolution, I was born . . .

The history of Folsom Prison dates to not too long after the Hangtown story would have happened. The well-off Livermore family was out to build a dam in the area and they contacted the State Prison Board looking for low-cost labor. The Board agreed to a trade: they got 350 acres and the Livermores got free labor. The prison has remained an institution (pun intended) ever since, and thanks to the song will likely stay that way forever. Less well known to the world, but probably more meaningful for our present purposes, is the fact that there's also a Johnny Cash Burger topped with bacon and blue cheese and finished with "Folsom Prison hot sauce."

Folsom has hosted a number of famous inmates, including funk bassist Rick James. Delving deep into bacon arcana, James turns out to have been a big fan of the stuff. During a 2002 interview, he talked about how he accrued a fortune worth more than $30 million. "Pork bellies I'm a fan of," he said, "because people, especially black people, whenever there's hard times, times of financial insecurity, black people going to eat some bacon. Some ham hocks, pork bellies." (If you're looking for stock tips, pharmaceuticals and holograms came up next on his list.)

As for Hangtown Fry, the dish is said to have originated at the now-defunct El Dorado Hotel, just across the street from the hanging tree. Legend has it that a miner rolled into town with gold from a fresh strike and ordered the saloonkeeper to serve up his most special dish. The cook offered a choice of three high-end options: oysters, eggs (hard to transport and hence costly) and bacon. The miner told him to toss all three into one dish, and Hangtown Fry was born.

It's a very versatile recipe—great for brunch, lunch or a light supper. Don't skimp on the egg quality—remember, they were a luxury in mid-nineteenth-century Hangtown and remain a key component of the dish, not just a way to hold the oysters and bacon together.

Since I almost never see single-serving recipes in cookbooks, I decided to design this one that way. But of course the quantities are easily increased for any number of diners. You can vary the number of oysters according to how much gold you've got in your pouch.

Ingredients:

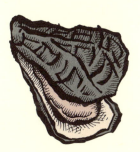

4 tablespoons oyster crackers, crushed

3 to 6 fresh oysters, shucked

5 ounces sliced bacon (about 2 to 3 slices), chopped

1½ teaspoons bacon fat

3 large eggs, beaten

⅛ teaspoon coarse sea salt

⅛ teaspoon freshly ground Tellicherry black pepper

Procedure:

Dredge the oysters in the cracker crumbs. Leave them resting for at least 10 minutes so that the crumbs bond with the oysters.

In a non-stick skillet, cook the bacon over medium heat until crisp. Remove from the pan, leaving the bacon fat. Reduce the heat a bit and add the additional measure of fat. When hot, add the oysters and cook for about 2 minutes, stirring gently, until the crumb coating is lightly browned.

Add the beaten eggs, salt and pepper, and stir gently. Add the bacon. Cook over low heat, stirring gently every 30 seconds or so, until the eggs are done as you like them.

Serve with San Francisco sourdough toast and "Folsom Prison Blues" playing in the background.

Serves 1 generously as a main dish, or 2 as a smaller side dish

Grits & Bits Waffles

This old Georgia dish has long been one of the most popular items on the Roadhouse brunch menu. The story is that the Dutch brought waffle irons here with them and that as they moved south from Manhattan they began to blend the local leftover grits that were so common into their waffles to make breakfast the next morning.

The dish really isn't very hard to make, but by bringing together the flavors of wheat, corn, bacon and maple syrup you really get a great, unique way to start the day. As always I'll recommend the Anson Mills grits, though other artisan offerings will also serve you well. The key is that the grits add flavor as well as texture to the dish. If you're into sorghum or cane syrups, you could certainly use either one instead of the maple. When it comes to the bacon, I'd go with one of the dry-cured offerings—Broadbent's, Edwards' or Benton's to stand up to all the other good flavors here.

Ingredients:

2 cups all-purpose flour
2 tablespoons sugar
1¼ teaspoons baking powder
2 cups water
6 tablespoons unsalted butter

1 cup Anson Mills (quick-cooking) grits
1 teaspoon coarse sea salt
4 eggs
1½ cups whole milk
1 pound sliced bacon (about 8 to 12 slices), cooked and coarsely chopped
6 ounces sharp cheddar (I'd recommend a nice two-year-old white cheddar
    like the one we get from Grafton Village in Vermont), shredded
Maple syrup and butter to taste for serving

Procedure:

In a mixing bowl, combine the flour, sugar and baking powder and set
aside.

In a saucepot, bring the water and butter to a simmer. Before the water
comes to a boil start adding the grits, stirring steadily until incorporated.
Add the salt and stir well. Reduce heat to low, cover and continue to simmer for 30 minutes, stirring occasionally. Add more water if needed.

While the grits are cooking, separate the eggs. Set the yolks aside in a
dish, and refrigerate the whites.

When the grits are done (you can always cook them longer than half an
hour—they'll continue to get creamier the longer you cook them), remove
them from the heat; transfer to a large mixing bowl and let cool to 110°F.
Stir the egg yolks into the grits one at a time, mixing well after each addition.

Add the milk and mix well.

Add the flour mixture, mixing until just combined.

Beat the cold egg whites in a mixer or with a hand beater to medium
peaks. Gently fold the whites into the batter and mix gently. Chill for at
least 1 hour prior to cooking. (Note: the batter can be made the night
before and stored in the refrigerator until you're ready to start cooking.)

When you're ready to eat, pour the batter into a preheated and well-
oiled Belgian-style waffle iron, and add a generous bit of chopped bacon
and shredded cheddar. (We use 1 cup of batter with ¼ cup each of bacon
and cheddar.) Close the waffle iron and cook until golden brown. Remove
the waffles from the iron and place on warm plates. Sprinkle more
chopped bacon and shredded cheddar over the top of the waffles. Serve
with good butter and real maple syrup.

Repeat until all the batter, chopped bacon and grated cheddar have
been used.

Serves 4 to 6 as a main dish

American Fried Bread

I learned this really simple dish from the book *Things Mother Used to Make*, published in 1914 by Lydia Maria Gurney. It's probably as down-to-earth, backwoods American cooking as you're going to get. You can serve it as is for breakfast or add a bit of sorghum syrup, maple syrup or molasses drizzled on top. It's also good sitting next to a salad for lunch or a light supper.

If you have reserved bacon fat on hand already you can just use that. If not, start by frying some bacon (let's say one slice per slice of bread) in a skillet. Remove the bacon, leaving the fat in the pan. (In tight times, the meat would have been used for other purposes later, but I'd say chop it and serve it on a salad alongside the bread.)

Keeping the fat hot, put slices of stale bread into the pan. You can of

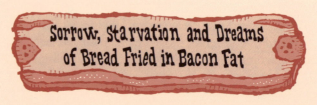

Sorrow, Starvation and Dreams of Bread Fried in Bacon Fat

This idea of bread cooked in bacon fat reminds me of a recipe "written" only in the mind of a WWI Italian POW, who I'm guessing would have given a lot for a go at a couple of slices of Mrs. Gurney's simple dish.

The POW was Second Lieutenant Giuseppe Chioni, who appears in John Dickie's history of Italian food, *Delizie*. Chioni, who spent months interned in a camp near the end of the war, wrote a book titled *Culinary Art*. It was never published; his family holds the original along with a few copies hand-published by his niece, who shared it with Dr. Dickie. From the sound of it, *Culinary Art* is very moving—almost heart-rending—and deeply informative. The essence of this is captured, I think, in the recipe for what Chioni calls Extravagant Soup, which Dickie describes as "a starving man's hallucinatory concoction of toasted bread soaked in lard with bacon and ham." In essence, an imagined Italian version of Mrs. Gurney's American Fried Bread.

course use most any bread, but my current favorite is a Bakehouse main-stay and long-time American classic. Around here we call it Roadhouse Bread, but it was known in the eighteenth and nineteenth centuries as Rye 'n' Injun, or, at times, Thirded Bread. It's made with a mix of rye, wheat and corn (hence the reference to thirds) and has a bit of molasses in it, as well. It's great on its own, and better still with bacon.

While the bread is frying add a couple of teaspoonfuls of either warm water or milk to the pan, and, if you like, a pinch of salt. When the bread is golden on the pan side, flip it and cook until it's nicely browned on the other side. As Mrs. Gurney said at the start of the last century, "This is a very appetizing dish."

Angels, Devils, Pigs . . . and a Nice Date with Bacon

These four little appetizers have been around a long time. They're great ways to bring bacon into a party setting without a whole lot of work. You can adjust the portions easily to fit whatever appetite, group size, budget or BQ (Sarah Katherine Lewis' "bacon quotient") you're working with.

ANGELS ON HORSEBACK

The angels, in this case, are oysters—their little frilly flaps get all fluffy and angelically winglike under the heat of the broiler. Angels on Horseback is often presented as fancy food, but it's in really basic books too, like V. M. Sherlock's *Apalachicola Seafood Recipes*—a small, softcover, brown pamphlety thing that I like a lot. Ms. Sherlock calls them by the unfancy name "broiled oysters," which just reinforces my belief that they're really a pretty darned down-to-earth way to eat. I like to use Arkansas long pepper bacon—it's got a nice bit of spice, but the moderate smoke level keeps the wood from completely overtaking the dish. Other bacons from the lighter smoke end of the spectrum, like Vande Rose, Nodine's and Nueske's, will also work well. As for the angels, any good oyster will work. I love Apalachicolas, which we bring to the Roadhouse regularly from Florida. I'll just share this note from Sherlock, who wrote that, "Throughout the ages, men have argued over the superior flavor of oysters of their regions, but until they have tasted the Apalachicola oyster, they're in no position to judge."

Ingredients:

8 oysters, shucked
4 slices bacon, cut in half crosswise

Procedure:

Heat the broiler.

Wrap a half-slice of bacon around each oyster and then run a toothpick through the whole thing to hold it together. Place on a baking sheet, run it under the broiler and cook until the bacon is done, giving it a turn halfway through. If you want the bacon well done you can cook it part way in a pan before wrapping it around the oysters.

Cook carefully: as V. M. Sherlock says, "Local appetites may differ but most will agree that you should never wash an oyster and never overcook one."

DEVILS ON HORSEBACK

These are made in the same manner as Angels, except that the oysters are replaced by dark Devils—in this case, prunes. Pork and prunes are a classic combination found in all sorts of big-flavored dishes from southwestern France, and this easy-to-make appetizer delivers that same wonderful flavor pairing to your guests in mere minutes! Of course you know already that I'm going to say you have to find really good ingredients to work with—my favorites are the prunes from Agen in France, but I don't think you can get them in the U.S. anymore. If you find a variety that's better than the standard supermarket grade, grab it. I like to make this dish with one of the smoky, dry-cured bacons to balance the sweetness of the dried fruit.

Ingredients:

8 really good prunes, pitted
4 slices bacon, cut in half crosswise

Procedure:

Heat the broiler.

Wrap a half-slice of bacon around each prune and then run a toothpick through the whole thing to hold it together. Place on a baking sheet, run it under the broiler and cook until the bacon is done, turning the "devils" halfway through the cooking. Again, if you want the bacon well done, you'll do better to cook it partially through on its own before you do the wrapping.

CLAM PIGS

This is the same dish as Angels on Horseback, but made with fresh clams instead of oysters. Gotta love the name, which I came across in Sherlock's Apalachicola cookbook!

Ingredients:

8 fresh clams, shucked
4 slices bacon, cut in half crosswise

Procedure:

Follow the instructions for Angels on Horseback, substituting the raw clams for oysters.

BACON DATES

Taking our passion for bacon a tad bit beyond the now-standard allusions to love and sex, it seems reasonable to go ahead and actually make a real life "date with bacon," don't you think? That said, I guess this recipe really is a literal as well as figurative date with bacon (or, actually, if you prepare the whole recipe, 16 dates with bacon). Of course there's really no limit, since you can multiply the recipe as many times as you like.

Bacon dates are a great little appetizer and extremely easy to make. If you're up for a "double date" you could serve it for dessert, too—I've never thought of using the same dish to both start and end a supper before, but given Americans' fondness for bacon it sort of makes sense to bacon-end the meal. I love the organic dates from Four Apostles in Bermuda Dunes, California. The sweet smokiness of the bacon with the buttery richness of their ripe dates and the spice of the long pepper gives this finger food a great bit of balance in its flavors.

Ingredients:

16 dates, pitted

8 slices bacon (we prefer these with the Broadbent bacon), cut in half crosswise

4 whole Balinese long peppers, quartered lengthwise

Procedure:

Heat the broiler.

Stuff each date with a sliver of long pepper, then wrap with a half-slice of bacon and secure with a toothpick. Place the bacon-wrapped dates on a baking sheet and broil 10 to 15 minutes or until the bacon is crisp, turning once. Keep an eye on them so they don't burn!

Remove from the oven once the bacon is done, let cool for a couple of minutes and serve while still warm.

Zingerman's Pimento Cheese

While everyone in the South knows this stuff at a level of intimacy my family would have reserved for chopped liver, it's still relatively unheard of up here in the North. Although pimento cheese doesn't have bacon in it, I'm giving you the recipe because it's so good with bacon *on it*—the two pair up nearly perfectly.

Small slices of toast, spread with pimento cheese and topped with a bit of crisp bacon and a leaf or two of celery make a superb appetizer. Pimento cheese sandwiches with bacon and tomato are terrific, too. I like them grilled, but they're actually very good toasted, as well. As for the bacon, I'd go for Broadbent's, Edwards' or Burgers': nice and meaty and smoky, but not so much so that they overpower the cheese.

We make a pimento cheese macaroni and cheese at the Roadhouse that's at its best topped with chopped bits of crisp bacon. This is also outstanding on a burger—not really melted, just softened up a bit from the heat of the meat. If that's where you're headed, I'd go for a couple of slices of Arkansas peppered bacon, along with a little bit of chopped celery leaf to lighten the whole thing up just a touch.

Ingredients:

> ½ pound sharp cheddar, coarsely grated (we use the two-year-old raw milk cheddar from Grafton Village)
> 1 cup mayonnaise (I prefer Hellmann's up here: out West the same mayo is sold under the brand name Best Foods)
> ¼ cup diced roasted red peppers
> ¾ teaspoon olive oil
> ¼ teaspoon freshly ground Tellicherry black pepper
> Scant ¼ teaspoon cayenne pepper, or to taste
> Pinch coarse sea salt

Procedure:

Fold all the ingredients together in a mixing bowl.
> Mix well.
> Eat.
> Repeat as regularly as you like. It's addictive: as more than one person

around here has said more than once, "It's kind of good on pretty much everything, isn't it?"

Serves . . . well, it's kind of hard to say. A real addict could probably consume this entire recipe in a single setting. Being more conservative, let's say it's enough to serve 8 as an appetizer. You'll probably have to test it on your family and friends to see how much they can eat!

Benedictine with Bacon

One day I was working my way through a Google search on Kentucky cooking when I came across something that said, "You know you're from Louisville when you think the rest of the world knows what Benedictine spread is." I'm not from Louisville and I definitely did not know what Benedictine spread was and without that tipoff I'd have assumed that Benedictine was just the French liqueur I used to drink too much of back when I first started working in restaurants. Of course, knowing nothing about an apparently key component of traditional Kentucky cooking, and being the curious and stubborn culinary history person and cook that I am immediately moved me to find out what it was.

The credit for inventing Benedictine spread goes to Jennie Benedict, a seemingly pretty powerful personality who studied with Fannie Farmer and went on to become one of Louisville's top caterers. She was the first woman to sit on a Board of Trade in the South. In 1902 she wrote a book called the *Blue Ribbon Cook Book*, in which she first described this spread. Over the last hundred years Benedictine has become to Louisville what paté is to Paris or baked beans are to Boston. Beyond that bit of background, I don't have a huge heck of a lot to tell you about Benedictine other than that it's really, really good and Louisvillians definitely do pretty uniformly seem to love it.

The first time I had it was at Lilly's, which is one of the best restaurants in the city. It wasn't on the menu but when I told Kathy Cary, the chef and owner, that I'd never eaten it she went straight to the kitchen and came back 10 minutes later with a plate of little Benedictine-filled finger sandwiches. I really liked the stuff, and I think pretty much anyone who likes cream cheese would like Benedictine. Every recipe calls for cream cheese, and they all have cucumber as well. Most have some onion. A few add other spices. The better the cream cheese and the cucumbers, the better it's going to be. Many locals add green food coloring, which I think was probably a pretty common ingredient back in the early years of the twentieth century (color was an important part of the way people approached food in that era of "scientific cooking," and the dishes of a meal were often color coded). Personally, I skip the green, but Kathy's husband quickly reminded me that rather surreal green color is the one I'd see in most supermarket deli cases.

Part of why I like our Benedictine so much is because I'm so smitten with the traditional, hand-made cream cheese from Zingerman's Creamery and this is a really good, regionally authentic way to eat it. I like to look at it as sort of a high-society, upper-South version of bagels with smoked salmon and cream cheese (slices of pork instead of salmon makes sense when you're hundreds of miles from the sea). The other reason is because it's really good with bacon—Kathy made that clear by topping each of the little sandwiches with a half slice of the stuff. Which is why it's in this book! I'd use Broadbent's or Father's to stay true to the Kentucky origins of the dish.

Ingredients:

1 large cucumber, peeled, seeded and grated
10 ounces Zingerman's Creamery cream cheese
2 tablespoons grated onion
Coarse sea salt to taste
Freshly ground Tellicherry black pepper to taste
4 slices bacon
4 slices good white bread

Procedure:

Drain the grated cucumber in a fine-mesh sieve. Combine the cucumber, cream cheese and onion in a food processor. Transfer to a bowl and add salt and pepper. Cover and let the spread set up for a couple of hours, refrigerated, to assimilate the flavors. Remove from the refrigerator about 30 minutes before serving.

When you're ready to serve, fry the bacon over medium heat until slightly crisp. While it's cooking, toast the bread. When the bacon's done, drain it (save that fat!) and cut the slices into quarters. When the toast is done, cut it into quarters as well, spread on the Benedictine and lay a bit of bacon on top. Serve on a genteel, socially acceptable platter!

Serves 4 as a side dish

Kieron's Grilled Plantain with Mustard and Bacon

When Kieron Hales, sous chef at the Roadhouse, first told me about this recipe, I thought it sounded a bit crazy. But, lo and behold, it's actually delicious. Kieron hails (sorry, couldn't resist) from England, but he learned this dish while he was working in Maine, from a Jamaican-born chef. The recipe works either on the grill or under the broiler, and you can make it with either ripe plantains or bananas. The latter will of course be somewhat sweeter, but both versions are quite good. Kieron recommends making it with a thickly sliced, very smoky bacon—consider Broadbent's, Edwards' or Benton's. It's also very good with the long pepper bacon from Arkansas—the tropical flavors of the plantains and bananas go well with the equatorial accent of the long pepper.

So yeah, it sounds strange, but tastes darned good!

Ingredients:

> 2 tablespoons dried mustard (preferably Colman's English)
> ¼ cup water
> 4 large ripe plantains (their skins will be mottled or black) or bananas
> 4 teaspoons freshly ground Tellicherry black pepper
> 8 to 12 slices bacon (each plantain requires 2 to 3 slices)

Procedure:

Soak a handful of wooden skewers in water for at least 1 hour or overnight. (I used 6-inch bamboo skewers, but toothpicks will work, as well.)

Mix the dried mustard and water together with a fork until it forms a paste. Let stand for 30 minutes so that the mustard's flavor can "bloom."

If using the grill, bring to medium-high heat. Alternatively, you can do the whole recipe, start to finish, under the broiler.

Rub each plantain with 1½ tablespoons of the mustard paste and sprinkle with 1 teaspoon pepper. Wrap each plantain in bacon slices, over-lapping by one-third the width of each slice as you go. Secure bacon to the plantain by inserting skewers crosswise and at angles as necessary.

Place the dressed plantains atop an oiled grill. If the plantains are very ripe, grill them for about 5 minutes, then turn and repeat on the other side for another 5 minutes. If the plantains are less ripe—with yellower

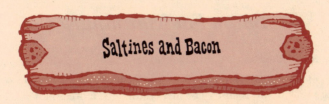

Saltines and Bacon

In a hurry, but just have to have that bacon fix? Here's a Southern sidebar courtesy of Mississippi native April McGreger, currently living in North Carolina. When we got to talking about this book, April 'fessed up that her favorite appetizer/snack was "bacon-wrapped Saltine crackers." Given that Saltines are often referred to only somewhat facetiously as "the traditional bread of the South," her confession surprised me more than it might have otherwise. Still, I can't say I'd ever given much thought to this combination. I'll have to do some experimenting to be sure which bacon goes best with the crackers. I should say, too, that although April likes to microwave them, the norm is apparently to eat one's pork-wrapped crackers at room temperature, "when they are the most crispy." (For info on April's very nice line of jams, chutneys and pickles check out http://www.farmersdaughterbrand.com/. For Saltines, see the cracker aisle at the supermarket.)

skins—you'll want to keep them on the grill longer (about 8 to 9 minutes per side).

Carefully remove the plantains to a baking sheet and place under the broiler for another 15 minutes, or until the bacon is crisped and the plantains are caramelized.

Take the pan from the broiler, carefully remove the skewers and cut the plantains into chunks. Serve hot, with some English mustard on the side for dipping.

Serves 4 as a side dish, or 10 to 12 as an appetizer

Bacon Fat Mayonnaise

When Jim Reische (pronounced "Reesh," as in "sheesh") was suggested as someone who'd be ideal to edit this book I can't say I was thinking much about recipes. For me, editing was more about good grammar, communication skills and the ability to deliver constructive criticism in ways that I could hear it well. Seeing as he's done all that and more I feel very good about his work. What I never thought about and certainly didn't expect were good ideas about cooking (nor did I anticipate that we'd share an affinity for Andre Williams!). Anyways, one of the first times we were meeting to talk publishing, Jim announced out of the blue that he used to make bacon fat mayonnaise. Both in content and in context he caught me so off guard that I had to pause and ponder the notion for a few minutes. But the more I thought about it, the more I liked the idea of it, and the recipe is even better "in person."

Here's Mr. Reische's recipe for bacon fat mayonnaise. It's pretty much good anywhere you'd want to put a little flavor of cured and smoked pork belly. Try a bit on a burger, a salad, dabbed onto deviled eggs or in potato salad. (For me it's a bit much on a BLT, but you can certainly try for yourself.) It's great as the dressing for a shrimp or chicken salad instead of your "regular" mayo. I've got it going into the bowl of North Carolina Fish Muddle (see page 183), the way you'd do rouille with bouillabaisse. Try it brushed onto grilled corn on the cob, then rolled in grated cheese, the way people in Mexico use regular mayonnaise. Basically . . . bacon fat mayonnaise is just plain good, a very civilized way to subtly (and invisibly to the naked eye) put the flavor of bacon into or onto most anything you're up for eating.

Ingredients:

5 egg yolks
1 tablespoon Dijon mustard
7 teaspoons freshly squeezed lemon juice
1¼ cups rendered bacon fat
½ teaspoon fine sea salt
Freshly ground Tellicherry black pepper to taste

Procedure:

Chill all the ingredients and utensils (including your mixing bowl) down to about 40°F. Don't skip this step or the mayonnaise may break.

Put the egg yolks, mustard, and 1½ teaspoons of the lemon juice into a blender or mixing bowl. Beat on high for 2 minutes, until well blended.

Add in the bacon fat (no need to add gradually if everything's properly chilled), continuing to beat until the mixture is thick. Depending on how thick and rich you like your mayonnaise you may or may not need the entire amount of fat.

Slowly blend in the remaining lemon juice, sea salt and pepper, whipping it pretty much continuously throughout. Adjust seasoning to taste.

The mayonnaise keeps for a couple of weeks in the refrigerator.

Yields about 2 cups

BFMLT:
The Bacon Fat Mayo, Lettuce
and Tomato Sandwich

This could be the sandwich of choice for borderline baco-tarians (see page 133 for more on this burgeoning movement). There's no bacon visible to turn off non-meat eaters, but the flavor still beckons softly from the creamy mayonnaise. The sandwich is actually delicious no matter how you feel about eating meat. Take 2 slices of toast and spread them with plenty of the bacon fat mayo, top with some nice leaf lettuce (or tender mustard greens, if you can find them) and slices of ripe tomato (or, if it's not tomato season, roasted red pepper). I like to add slices of grilled zucchini, as well—the smokiness of the grill brings out the subtle smokiness of the bacon fat.

Emma Dencklau's
Iowa German Potato Salad

This recipe first came up courtesy of historian and long-time Zinger-man's customer Leo Landis, whom I met many years ago when he was working at the Henry Ford Museum in Dearborn. Leo moved back to his native Iowa a few years ago, but we've continued to correspond: I asked for his help in preparing a special "Foods of Iowa" dinner at the Roadhouse, and in return he shared many lovely little bits of Iowa history and culture, one of which was this great bacon-powered potato salad.

The Dencklau recipe dates to the early part of the twentieth century and probably goes back to older roots in Germany. Emma's family arrived here from Germany at the turn of the last century. According to the 1920 census she was born in 1902 in Webster County, about 100 miles north of Des Moines. Today the trip is about an hour and a half by car, but back then it would have been roughly two days each way on horseback. Looking down the census page you can see how many families in the area were of German origin, so it's not surprising that potato salads like this were and are very common. Leo got the recipe from the grandson of the woman to whom it's credited, which means it's basically third-generation American by this point.

The vinegar is a key ingredient, whose quality is integral to the flavor of the finished dish. As I've said many times, I'm very high on the cider vinegar we get from Pierre Gingras in Quebec. It's made from hand-picked apples, no windfalls, no dregs, then aged for over two years in oak barrels. In this dish it adds that lively vinegar zip, but because Gingras' is so well-made and its flavor so well-rounded, the flavor of the finished dish is lively without seeming overly sharp. Rather than using tap water I used the cook-ing water from the potatoes, both because the starch in the water helps binds the sauce and because it brings its own flavor to the salad.

Emma's exact recipe is below. I used the Nueske's applewood-smoked bacon, since its roots are—as were Emma's—both German and Midwest-ern. I've kept the original, large quantities because they more accurately reflect the way dishes were cooked back in Emma's day. All the ingredients are portioned in nice round numbers, so you can easily halve or quarter the amounts if you want.

I personally don't love sweet salads, so I when I make this at home I add almost none of the sugar that Emma calls for. By contrast I probably put in a bit more freshly ground black pepper. Regardless, the finished salad is darned delicious—very rich, but lightened on the palate by the goodly dose of vinegar.

Ingredients:

4 pounds potatoes (I prefer Yukon Golds or German butterballs because they're delicious and buttery in their own right, and also because they absorb the bacon fat so beautifully)

1 pound sliced Nueske's or comparable bacon (about 8 to 12 slices)

1 large onion, coarsely chopped

2 tablespoons flour

½ cup cider vinegar

2 tablespoons sugar (optional)

Procedure:

Steam the potatoes in their skins over salted water for 30 minutes or until well-cooked and fork tender. Remove them from the heat and allow to cool, reserving 1¼ cups of the cooking water.

Fry the bacon over medium heat until nearly crisp but still bendable, then remove it from the pan and cut it into 1-inch pieces. Leave the fat in the pan.

Reduce heat to low and add the onion to the pan. Cook over low heat until soft, stirring occasionally.

Raise heat to medium. Sift the flour over the onions, then stir steadily for about 5 minutes to make a roux. The flour and fat should become well bound and very lightly brown in color.

Slowly add the cider vinegar to the roux, stirring steadily until the sauce thickens. Repeat with the potato water, again stirring constantly until the sauce is thickened. Add the sugar if you like and, again, mix well. Remove from the heat.

Cut the cooked potatoes into 1-inch cubes and add them to the sauce along with the bacon pieces. Mix gently, but well.

Serve immediately, while the salad is still warm. It also keeps well in the refrigerator—you can serve it the next day and it's still quite good, either cold or reheated.

Serves 4 to 6 as a main course, or 8 as a side dish

Dandelion Green Salad
with Hot Bacon Dressing, Two Ways

This recipe came courtesy of Francois Vecchio, one of the most knowledgeable people on the subject of cured pork I've ever met. Once you know his background, you can see why. He grew up in Switzerland in the 1940s ("It was war outside of our little Swiss world," he recalled). His father's father was Piemontese, but moved to Geneva where he became a butcher. The roots are equally strong on his mother's side. "My gran'pa," he told me, "had the best restaurant in Geneva, Restaurant Chouard. He had learned his trade in London, Aswan, Davos and the Black Forest."

After years of traveling the world while apprenticing as a butcher, Francois ended up in the family meat business based in Ticino. Eventually he moved to the States, where he has been involved in a wide range of efforts to cure traditional European salamis, hams and, of course, bacon. He's now retired to Alaska, after living in California for decades. Alaska, Francois says, harkens back to his youth in the Alps—"It's probably that old addiction, which makes me choose Alaska," he explained, "the space here was in the mountains, rocks and glaciers."

Tall, highly talented, incredibly intelligent and very humble, he speaks softly, slowly and deliberately with what I think is a poetic-sounding Swiss-Italian accent. He's probably the first person I call when I need help with any question about cured meat. While he knows the science of charcuterie inside and out, Francois also loves the aesthetics of cooking and eating good food, and he can and does speak to all those subjects with great passion.

All of which, I guess, explains why I sent him an early draft of this book. Given his technical expertise, I expected to get back some corrections on what I'd written about curing techniques. What he sent instead were childhood memories, an enthusiasm for good eating, and this recipe, a simple one that I'd never run into before. Aside from the fact that it tastes really good, it's pretty clear that it summons strong memories of his childhood in the mountains—memories that he has carried across two continents.

"The rite of spring," Francois set out, "is that the dandelions are the first to grow. As soon as the season allows I pick them as a bunch, like a bouquet, cutting just below the collar into the bitter root; sometimes I find some growing through some mulch, they are longer, whiter and sweeter."

(*The Pennsylvania Dutch Cookbook*, published in 1961, recommends that you "never use dandelion greens that have begun to flower, because they are apt to be bitter." More on the Pennsylvania Dutch in a minute.) "Washing," Francois went on, "is a chore and some sand always sticks around to the plate. The miracle occurs when on a first drizzling of balsamic vinegar and some brown mustard, I pour the hot rendering and sizzling and crisp diced bacon." "My grandmother always claimed that it purges the liver of all the winter miasms," he added. I don't have data to support his grandmother's claim, but I do know the salad is very good.

Interestingly, as we were working to transform Francois' notes into culinary reality, the woman who was doing our testing—Jean Henry—shared her own experience out of the German tradition here in the U.S., bringing the bacon story full circle. "I grew up with a Pennsylvania Dutch version of this salad," she emailed the same evening she saw Francois' version. "We also went out with our Pennsylvania Dutch babysitter and gathered the greens, before they were too large and bitter. We also gathered up the rosette of new leaves in a bunch and cut to the crown with a paring knife run round it. I always thought this was to prevent the plant from returning and to get all the smallest leaves—the Pennsylvania Dutch are always very efficient. We later cut off the root stalk. We triple washed the greens in the deep sink then spun them dry while the bacon cooked. And we always picked the greens as close to mealtime as possible."

The recurrence of culinary patterns—in this case, a few thousand miles and probably 30 years apart—always catches my interest. Jean's family is not alone in its love for this dish: many Pennsylvania Dutch trace their roots back to the Swiss Germans. Having now been alerted to its popularity, I've come across many similar recipes, some calling for an astoundingly high ratio of 1 pound of bacon to 2 pounds of greens! Those were the days!

As always, the variants make slight allowances—perhaps "adaptations" is more appropriate—for the availability of local ingredients. "The only difference," Jean demurred, "is that in our version we used apple cider vinegar not Balsamic, the mustard was sweet German not Dijon, and the bacon was apple smoked, not pancetta." Some of the Pennsylvania Dutch add eggs, as Jean's family did raw, or others do in hard-boiled form. The salad, she added, was eaten, "only for a week or two each year in the spring, but during that time in more traditional households it was served at every dinner (which was eaten at midday) and often supper (in the evening, which we called 'dinner') too." In talking to her mother about her memories, Jean was reminded that, "Dandelion salad was to be eaten on Maundy Thursday (the Thursday before Easter, and the day of the Last Supper) to keep away illness the following year. This," she said, "was as sensible as it was superstitious because the greens are full of the vitamin C (plus calcium and other vitamins) largely absent from the winter diet." It also aligns with what Francois Vecchio's grandmother used to say many years ago about those mysterious miasms.

As always, the better your ingredients the better your end result. The vinegar is especially important—I went out on a limb and made it luxuriously with a *very* good traditional balsamic vinegar and unsurprisingly it was exceptionally delicious. My training told me to mix the vinegar and mustard in advance to assure a smooth texture, but I asked Francois twice to be sure and he held firm that his family sprinkled the vinegar and spooned the mustard onto the greens one after the other, and then added the hot bacon fat just the way it's written below.

I try to imagine Francois as a kid up in the mountains every time I eat this. The salad's very good, and so are the images.

Ingredients:

8 ounces (about 4 slices) pancetta, diced
8 ounces fresh dandelion greens, stems removed
2 teaspoons Dijon mustard
3 tablespoons balsamic vinegar
Coarse sea salt to taste
Freshly ground Tellicherry black pepper to taste

Procedure:

Fry the pancetta over medium heat until crisp.

While the pancetta is cooking wash the greens, then spin or pat them very dry. Place them in a warm, but not hot, serving bowl.

When the pancetta is done, immediately pour it and all its drippings straight from the skillet over the greens. If you need more fat, you can add a bit of olive oil. Toss immediately so that the hot fat wilts the greens a bit. Spoon the mustard onto the greens, then sprinkle on the vinegar, then toss again. Add salt and pepper to taste, toss one more time and serve right away.

(Francois adds, "My grandma even tossed a spoon of flour on the greens to soak more of the extra hot fat, it was fabulous but probably hard to convey to today's consumers." Feel free to try it at home.)

Serves 2 as a main course, or 4 as a side dish

FOR THE PENNSYLVANIA DUTCH VERSION:

Substitute an American smoked bacon for the pancetta—Jean Henry recommends the Arkansas peppered bacon. For the dressing, whisk together all of the ingredients: 2 teaspoons of a sweet, smooth German-style mustard, 1 egg, a teaspoon or so of sugar, 3 tablespoons of good apple cider vinegar, about 2 teaspoons of the bacon fat, and salt and pepper. Pour the dressing over the dandelion greens immediately and eat the dressed salad while it's still warm.

BLT in a Bowl

Basically, it's everything great about the sandwich but served in a bowl, inverting the normal ratios of a BLT in order to make the lettuce and tomato the feature. Use good cider vinegar—I'm very partial to the oak-barrel aged one we get from Pierre Gingras in Quebec, or the one from Albert Katz out in California.

Ingredients:

8 ounces sliced bacon (about 4 to 6 slices)
1 slice good bread of your choice, preferably a bit stale, cut into 1-inch cubes
6 ounces good greens, washed, well dried and coarsely chopped (I like
    mustard greens, but of course any good lettuce will work)
1 big or 2 medium or 4 small ripe, in-season tomatoes, cut into ½-inch chunks
1 ripe avocado, cubed
1 tablespoon cider vinegar
Coarse sea salt to taste
Plenty of freshly ground Tellicherry black pepper to taste
1 tablespoon white vinegar
2 eggs

Procedure:

Fry the bacon in a skillet over medium heat. Remove the bacon from the pan, leaving the fat. Add the bread cubes and stir well. Keep cooking, stirring occasionally, until golden brown on all sides.

Meanwhile, put the greens in a pair of chilled salad bowls and top with the tomatoes and avocado. Sprinkle with salt, pepper and cider vinegar and toss well.

Add white vinegar and two inches of cold water to a sauce pan and bring to a boil. Reduce the heat and carefully break the eggs directly into the liquid. Cook until the eggs are lightly poached. Turn off the heat and allow the eggs to rest in the warm liquid.

Chop the bacon and add it to the salad bowls. Sprinkle with the croutons and remaining bacon fat and toss well. (If there's not enough bacon fat for your liking, add a glug from your stash or augment it with a good olive oil.)

Gently remove the eggs from the pan with a slotted spoon and spoon one over the top of each salad.

Option: Drop the egg (figuratively) from the recipe and substitute a handful of blue cheese broken into small bits. I like to put the cheese on the salad before I add the croutons, so that the heat of the hot bread softens the cheese.

Serves 2 as a main course, or 4 as a side dish

Wilted Salad

A great all-American dish dating back to the Colonial era, wilted salad uses bacon fat as the basis for a dressing in much the same way that olive oil is used to dress greens in the Mediterranean. The heat of the bacon dressing wilts the greens—hence the name. April McGreger, who grew up with bacon fat as the basis for a lot of her family's food, told me that they called this "killt lettuce"—because the lettuce is "slain" by the hot fat, not because of any connection to Scottish menswear. The bacon's flavor is a big part of the dish, so use whatever variety strikes your fancy. Because the fat will solidify once it cools, the dressing must be served warm.

Ingredients:

6 ounces mixed greens, washed and dried
6 ounces sliced bacon (about 3 to 4 slices)
2 scallions (greens and whites), thinly sliced
2 tablespoons cider vinegar
½ teaspoon sugar
Coarse sea salt to taste
2 ounces cheddar cheese, diced (optional)
¼ cup walnuts or hickory nuts, lightly toasted and chopped (optional)
Freshly ground Tellicherry black pepper to taste

Procedure:

Place the greens in a large, heat-proof serving bowl.

Fry the bacon in a heavy-bottomed skillet over medium heat until crisp. Remove from the skillet, drain and chop it. Reserve about 4 tablespoons of fat in the skillet (augment with a glug from your backup supply if necessary).

Add the sliced scallions to the pan and cook for a minute. Pour in the cider vinegar, sugar and a pinch of salt. Stir well and boil lightly for a minute.

If you're using cheese or toasted nuts, distribute them over the greens. Pour the hot dressing over the top, toss well and sprinkle with the bits of cooked bacon and plenty of fresh pepper. Serve warm.

Serves 2 as a main course, or 4 as a side dish

Dutch Bacon and Gouda Potato Salad

We've been making this simple salad at the Deli for many years now. It's a great side dish, or you can serve it over mixed greens for a nice lunch. It makes for a nice picnic dish because you can prepare it a day ahead if you like so there's less to do the day of the event. I like to do it with Nueske's applewood-smoked because the sweet smoky flavor of their bacon complements the cheese so nicely. The gouda should be a full-flavored farmstead cheese, of modest maturity (say 6 months or so at the least). I like to sprinkle the whole thing with the either cumin or caraway seeds but I've left them as optional since some folks object to seed eating of that sort.

Ingredients:

3 pounds potatoes (preferably Yukon Gold or German butterballs)
10 ounces sliced bacon (about 5 to 7 slices)
1¼ cups mayonnaise
½ cup Dijon mustard
6 scallions, sliced thin
½ pound Gouda cheese, cut into ¼-inch cubes
Coarse sea salt to taste
Freshly ground Tellicherry black pepper to taste
1 tablespoon cumin seed or caraway seed, toasted (optional)

Procedure:

Steam the potatoes until tender, about 25 minutes.

While the potatoes are cooking, fry the bacon in a skillet over medium heat until done. Remove the bacon from the pan, leaving the fat.

When the potatoes are done, remove them from the pot and cut them into ½-inch cubes while still hot.

Pour the hot fat over the potatoes and mix well. Let the mixture rest for about 30 minutes. The potatoes will absorb the fat while cooling enough to be mixed with the mayonnaise. Chop the bacon into ½-inch pieces.

Combine the mayonnaise and mustard and dress the cooled potatoes. Add the bacon and scallion. Toss gently to mix. Add the cheese and mix well again. Season with salt and pepper to taste.

Sprinkle with cumin or caraway seeds as a garnish if desired.

Serves 6 as a side dish

North Carolina Fish Muddle

"Bacon makes the soup"
—Provençal saying

I'm not sure how I first heard of this dish, but it has become one of my favorite ways to cook fish stew over the years. It's clearly in the same culinary tradition as all the one-pot seafood stews made anywhere near the ocean—something between a thickened bouillabaisse with bacon and a fish-dominated, lightly tomato-based chowder.

Although I'd always seen this billed as "Outer Banks Fish Muddle" I was steered straight by Elizabeth Wiegand, author of the *Outer Banks Cookbook*. "Muddles are done both at the coast and up rivers, so some sources say," she explained. "However, I've always considered them INNER coast." What she's saying makes good sense. As she pointed out quickly, while it makes a great summer getaway and provides for some fine fishing, the thin strip of land that is the Outer Banks has never been a good place for raising the pigs from which the bacon for this fish stew comes.

(As a pig-related side note, Elizabeth also shared with me that back in the nineteenth century the North Carolinian upper crust built homes on the Outer Banks, then ferried all their possessions across the bay: servants, supplies, pigs and cows all came over. The livestock liked to root under the houses, which in and of itself isn't a terrible thing. But the small holes in the floors of the Outer Banks houses, which allowed floodwaters to drain, also allowed the smell of the animals to permeate their interiors. The latticework that became so typical of houses in this area was originally installed to keep the animals and aromas away from the living quarters.)

Most recipes for muddle rely on rockfish, so called because the fish hang out near rocks. You may know them as striped bass, which fisherman refer to as "strip-ers." What I didn't know until speaking with Elizabeth is that they're also known along the Carolina coast as "Mr. Pajama Pants" because of the horizontal black stripes that run up their hindquarters. Better still, some folks call them "squid hounds" for their propensity to chase squid, one of their favorite foods. The spring and fall are prime striper seasons—one theory of muddle making being that people had end of the year get-togethers to cook up the new season's fish (remember, the slaughter took place around New Year's, as well).

There are a few thousand versions of muddle. In part because it's so good, and in part because this book is about bacon, I've put the pork more out front than some other cooks might have done. With that in mind, I prefer to feature the bigger flavors of an Edwards' or Benton's. I use a mixture of different fish for greater complexity of flavor and texture, but it's certainly great made exclusively with striped bass, as well.

The sliced bread isn't in many recipes but it's a great way to bring more bacon flavor to the dish. Elizabeth reminded me that many Southerners would use Saltines, which are, of course, widely considered a "traditional" bread down below the Mason-Dixon line. I have eggs listed as optional—most recipes don't use them but I think they're delicious. I've old references to doing the same in various versions, including one from Beth Tartan's 1955 classic book, *North Carolina Cookery*.

Muddle is mostly considered a main dish, but you could certainly serve it in smaller portions as a soup course.

Ingredients:

8 ounces (about 4 to 6 slices) bacon, diced

2 medium onions, diced

1 large leek, washed well and thinly sliced

1 large or 2 medium carrots, diced

2 stalks celery, diced

1 clove garlic, minced

1 bay leaf

2 pounds fresh plum tomatoes, chopped (in the off-season I'd suggest using good-quality canned)

An additional 4 ounces bacon, in a single chunk

1 tablespoon chopped fresh thyme leaf

¼ teaspoon hot red pepper flakes (I like the Marash red pepper flakes from Turkey)

2 tablespoons parsley, chopped, rinsed and squeezed dry

4 cups fish stock

½ pound pollock or other inexpensive white ocean fish, cut into 1-inch pieces

1½ pounds waxy potatoes (I like Yukon Golds), cut into ½-inch dice

1 pound striped bass or other full-flavored ocean fish, cut into 1-inch
    chunks
1 pound cod or other flaky white ocean fish, cut into 1-inch chunks
Coarse sea salt to taste
Freshly ground Tellicherry black pepper to taste
6 eggs (optional)
6 slices good crusty bread
3 to 4 tablespoons reserved hot bacon fat
Bacon fat mayonnaise (optional, see page 172)

Procedure:

Brown the diced bacon over medium heat in a soup kettle or large Dutch
oven until crisp. Remove and set aside. Remove the 3 to 4 tablespoons of
drippings and reserve for garnish, leaving the rest in the pot. (If you don't
have enough fat in the pan, feel free to add a glug from the jar you've now
started saving . . . right?)

Sauté the onion, leek, carrot and celery in the fat until soft. Stir gently
to be sure they don't stick.

Add the garlic and bay leaf and cook for 2 more minutes.

Add the tomatoes, bacon chunk, thyme, red pepper and parsley and
cook over medium high for 10 to 15 minutes, until the tomatoes release
their juices and begin to reduce.

Add the fish stock, pollock pieces and potatoes and bring to a strong
simmer. Reduce heat to medium low. Simmer, uncovered, for about 2
hours. The muddle should be the texture of a moderately thick vegetable
soup, so add more water if needed.

Remove the bacon chunk and set aside for future use. (At this point,
the stew can be cooled and held in the refrigerator overnight, to be finished the following day. If you do so, be sure to bring the broth back to a
strong simmer before continuing.)

Add the striped bass and cod, submerging them in the stewing juices,
and bring back to a low boil.

Simmer for 5 to 8 minutes, until fish is just done. Add salt and pepper
to taste. The stew should be thick and savory.

If using the eggs either poach them in a separate pot or do as I do
and just crack them gently into the muddle when it starts to simmer, after
you've added the final pieces of fish.

When the stew is just about ready, toast the bread. Rub each slice with
some of the reserved bacon fat.

Warm the bowls in the oven. Ladle in the muddle and top with a slice of the toast. Place one of the poached eggs in each bowl. Sprinkle with the diced bacon.

You can also treat the muddle like a Marseillaise bouillabaisse by spooning a dollop of bacon fat mayonnaise atop the toast as a rouille. (It's delicious!)

Serves 4 to 6 as a main course, or 8 as a side dish

Bluefish Fried in Bacon with Blue Grits

Bluefish is one of my all-time favorite foods. But once you get off the East Coast it seems like hardly anyone knows it. This is a simple preparation, it has a great name, it's pretty eye-catching on the plate and, most importantly, it tastes extremely terrifically good. I made it with the really superb, organic, stone-ground blue grits that we get from Glenn Roberts' Anson Mills in South Carolina. Given that the old corn varieties ranged in color from white to red to yellow to blue and most everything in between (or even all on one cob—try Glenn's multi-colored "speckled grits" too!), blue grits really aren't all that strange.

It'll mess up your all-blue color scheme, but this is also good with cooked greens on the side. To get back into the blue end of the spectrum you can follow with fresh blueberries and a dollop of fresh whipped cream (no bacon) for dessert!

FOR THE GRITS

Ingredients:

Since the cooking time is the most challenging element of this recipe, feel free to prepare a larger portion than you actually need and save some for later.

    4 cups cold water
    1 cup Anson Mills blue grits
    ½ teaspoon coarse sea salt

Procedure:

Heat the water in a heavy four-quart stockpot. Start mixing in the grits while the water warms up, stirring regularly—I find it infinitely easier to get lump-free grits this way. Add salt and stir well.

Bring to a boil, then reduce the heat as low as possible. Stir a few more times, cover and cook on low for as long as you can—a good 2 to 4 hours—the long, slow cooking releases the starches and makes the grits really creamy. Once you get them cooking there's really nothing to do but stir every 15 minutes or so.

FOR THE FISH

When the grits are good and creamy and you're ready to eat, you can start the fish.

Ingredients:

> 4 ounces sliced bacon (about 2 to 3 slices)(I like the dry-cured Edwards' bacon for this one)
> 2 (½ pound) fillets fresh bluefish
> Coarse sea salt to taste
> Freshly ground Tellicherry black pepper to taste
> Extra virgin olive oil (optional)

Procedure:

Fry the bacon in a heavy-bottomed skillet over moderate heat. Remove the bacon from the pan and drain, leaving the fat in the pan.

Add the fish to the still-hot bacon fat in the skillet, skin side down (I think the skin is the best part!). Cook the fish until the skin is browned, then flip and cook quickly on the other side. If you need more fat, add a glug from your reserves or use a bit of olive oil.

While the fish is cooking, chop the bacon coarsely and set aside.

When the fish is almost done, set the grits into a couple of warm bowls. Place the fish on top, skin side down. Sprinkle the fat over the whole thing and top with salt, pepper and chopped bacon.

Serves 2 as a main course

Mac and Grease
(a.k.a. Māc 'n' Bacon)

I really struggled over what to name this dish. Meg Noori, our Ojibway expert (mentioned a hundred pages or so ago), calls it "Mac and Grease," which doesn't exactly whet my appetite. On the other hand, being prone to stupid puns and rhymes and such, I couldn't let go of the sound of "Māc 'n' Bacon": if you pronounce it with a long "a" it comes out as "Makin' Bacon," and . . . Anyway, you probably don't care, but there you go. Since it's Meg's dish, her name for it comes first and I've subsumed mine into parentheses.

Naming nonsense aside, this dish is actually one of the best things I've eaten in ages. As obvious as it seems, I'd certainly never had it or even considered it until Meg told me how it was a big part of her Native American upbringing here in Michigan. Once I had the dish on my mind it was hard to get it out. I made it the next day. And, because it was so good, the day after that as well.

In essence this is sort of an American pasta carbonara, sans the egg. Meg's adaptation is historically interesting: here you have Native Americans regularly eating two ingredients that weren't native to pre-Columbian cooking. And the obvious consonance with Italians' use of olive oil on pasta is too obvious to ignore.

It's so simple and so quick to prepare, I think this is a dish that could give "fast food" a good name!

Ingredients:

½ pound really good macaroni (I swear by the Martelli family's)
8 ounces sliced bacon (about 4 to 6 slices)(I like Benton's because the simplicity of the dish gets its full smokiness out front)
Coarse sea salt to taste
Freshly ground Tellicherry black pepper to taste

Procedure:

Bring a large pot of water to a boil. Add lots of salt, then pasta. Stir well.

While the pasta is cooking, fry the bacon in a large skillet over medium heat until done. Remove the bacon from the pan, reserving the hot fat in the skillet. Chop the bacon and stand by. As soon as the pasta is almost *al dente*, drain it well and add it to the skillet along with the bacon. Toss well and cook for another minute or two, so that the grease really cooks into the macaroni. Season with salt and plenty of black pepper to taste. Serve immediately in hot bowls.

Optional additions:

"Enh," Meg wrote me a day or so after she'd sent the original recipe (the word means "yes" in Ojibway). "Try the mac and grease with a few big garden tomatoes cut into 1-inch cubes." It's incredibly simple—just chunks of really good tomato tossed into the hot bacon fat for a minute or two with some salt before the pasta goes into the skillet. "The tomatoes," she said, should "get hot but not saucy, if you know what I mean." I did, and I made the dish and it was, again, in its simplicity, really, really good. Of course it's only worth doing when the tomatoes are in season. The rest of the year you could gussy up your Mac and Grease by tossing in chopped vegetables or greens of most any sort, and cooking until they're somewhere between soft and golden brown. Thinking more exotically, I want to throw chopped hickory nuts on top, too. You, of course, can do whatever you like. Like most pasta dishes, this one lends itself to hundreds of variations.

Serves 2 as a main course, or 4 as a side dish

South Carolina Red Rice

This recipe is classic cookery from the South Carolina (and actually Georgia as well) coast. A staple dish of the Lowcountry—one of North America's most interesting and important regional cuisines— you can probably find six hundred different recipes for red rice in Southern cookbooks. The dish uses meat—here it's bacon, of course—as an accent, so that you're eating the same sort of rice and vegetable-dominated diet that one might get in the Mediterranean (but, again, using bacon fat in place of olive oil). Glenn Roberts from Anson Mills says he gives credit for this dish to émigré Sephardic Jews, although they probably weren't doing it with bacon as nearly everyone does today. In her book about Southern Jewish cookery, *Matzo Ball Gumbo*, Marcie Ferris shares a recipe that uses Kosher salami instead!

If you make Red Rice with Uncle Ben's, out-of-season tomatoes and supermarket bacon the dish is going to be fairly unremarkable. For me, the Anson Mills Carolina Gold is key to making the dish as exceptional as it can be. It's a South Carolina low-yield, high-flavor rice varietal that dates back to the nineteenth century, so it's the right rice to use for both authenticity and excellence of eating. Organically grown, field-ripened, custommilled to retain all of the germ and most of the bran, it's exceptionally flavorful stuff. You can certainly work with other varieties (most people do), but remember that, a) the flavor and texture of Carolina Gold is really something special, and b) you'll need to adjust your cooking times and liquid-to-rice ratio a bit.

As to which pork to use, I like the Arkansas peppered bacon, but Sam Edwards' dry-cured would be excellent, too. As in all Lowcountry cooking, the rice should really be in distinctive, individual grains when you're done, rather than the creamily bound-together form you'd get from Italian risotto.

Ingredients:

2 cups Anson Mills Carolina Gold rice
4 medium tomatoes or 1 (14.5-ounce) can
    whole peeled tomatoes with their juice
8 ounces sliced Arkansas peppered bacon
    (about 4 to 6 slices)
1 small onion, chopped

2 cups chicken broth (preferably homemade or one of the better commercial
   brands: you may not end up using it all, but any leftover broth can be
   cooled and used later in the week)
Coarse sea salt to taste
Freshly ground Tellicherry black pepper to taste

Procedure:

Wash the rice in cold water three times, or until the water runs clear. This
keeps the grains from sticking together.

Halve the tomatoes and squeeze the juice into a medium bowl. If you're
using canned tomatoes, use the juice from the can. You'll want about 2
cups of liquid for cooking the rice, so top off the tomato juice with chicken
broth if necessary.

Chop the tomatoes and set aside. You should have about 1 cup.

Fry the bacon in a heavy-bottomed stockpot over moderate heat until
almost crisp. Remove from the pot and drain. (You'll want about ¼ cup
bacon grease, so add a bit from your stash if needed.)

Reduce heat slightly and add the chopped onion. Sauté, stirring occasionally, until nicely caramelized—about 20 minutes.

When the onions are just about ready, bring the broth and tomato
juice to a boil in a medium-sized pan and reduce to a low simmer. If you're
working with unsalted broth, add 1 teaspoon coarse salt.

When the onions are caramelized, raise the heat in the pot a bit, add
the rice and stir well. Sauté for a couple of minutes, stirring constantly,
until the rice is very hot and shiny.

Stir the chopped tomatoes into the rice and cook for several minutes,
stirring constantly.

Add the simmering broth into the rice, stirring well. Bring to a boil,
cover the pan, reduce heat to low and cook for 10 minutes. Turn off the
heat. (And *don't* pick up that lid to look, either, OK?) Let stand, covered,
for another 10 minutes.

While the rice is cooking, chop the bacon.

Remove the lid from the rice pot, add the bacon and stir gently. Flavor
with salt and a generous dose of freshly ground black pepper, fluff with a
fork and serve.

Serves 4 to 6 as a main dish

Oyster and Bacon Pilau

This is a dish that's been at the top of my cooking regimen of late. It's so good, and so easy to do, that I just keep making it over and over again. You know from the name that the dish has oysters in it. By contrast, the word "pilau" may not be one you recognize right off, although when I tell you that the other main ingredient in the recipe is rice, you'll pretty quickly realize that pilau is likely an early American version of "pilaf."

The South Carolina coast is as famous for its rice pilaus as eastern Spain is for paella (for more on the subject see John Martin Taylor's great *Lowcountry Cooking*). The name is pronounced either "PUHR-LOE" or "pi-LOE." No one is quite sure how these now-typical rice dishes were brought to the coast of South Carolina, but they've been there for centuries. Karen Hess' reissue of the classic *The Carolina Rice Kitchen* includes dozens of pilaus and comparable rice dishes. Her theory is that Persian Jews brought the technique to Provence. When the Huguenots later fled France for colonial Carolina, their numbers included quite a few *converso* (secret) Jews who carried these rice dishes with them to the New World.

South Carolina is, of course, quintessential rice country—everyone I've talked to who grew up there says (usually with great gravity) something like, "You have to understand, we eat rice at *every* meal. Breakfast, lunch and dinner. If there's no rice on the table, it's not a meal."

I was inspired to make this version with oysters while flipping through Matt and Ted Lee's *Southern Cookbook*. We'd been selling huge amounts of oysters at the Roadhouse and had the new-crop Carolina Gold rice (it arrives in late November or early December) in at the same time, so it was sort of an obvious choice. Below is my adaptation of the Lee brothers' recipe.

I like the Arkansas peppered bacon for its spice, or the Edwards' for its intensity, but you can follow wherever your taste buds lead you. Adapt at will!

Ingredients:

8 ounces sliced bacon (about 4 to 6 slices)
1 pint shucked oysters, plus liquor
1 teaspoon extra virgin olive oil
1 medium onion, diced

1 stalk celery, diced

1 cup Anson Mills Carolina Gold rice

2 cups chicken broth

1 teaspoon coarse sea salt, plus more to taste

1 teaspoon freshly ground Tellicherry black pepper, plus
more to taste

Procedure:

Rinse the rice 3 times, or until the water runs clear. Drain.

Fry the bacon in a skillet over medium heat until crisp. Remove from pan, drain and chop.

Add the oysters to the pan, leaving liquor aside for now. Turn the oysters gently to cook on all sides—about 2 minutes total, but do not overcook. Remove from the pan with a slotted spoon and set aside.

Add olive oil to the pan. Toss in the onion, celery and 1 teaspoon each of salt and pepper. Cook until soft.

Add the rice to the pan and toast lightly with the vegetables for 2 minutes, stirring gently but constantly.

Add the oyster liquor and chicken broth. Stir to combine. Bring to a slow boil, then cover and reduce heat to low.

Cook for 12 minutes. Turn off heat and allow rice to steam for another 12 minutes.

Uncover. Add the oysters and chopped bacon and gently fold into the rice so as not to break up the grains. Add salt to taste. Serve immediately, with lots of freshly ground pepper.

Serves 2 as a main course

Anson Mills Mush and Bacon

This is one of those dishes that I'd seen mentioned many times in old cookbooks, but never actually took the time to make. It sounds so simple and unexciting that I wasn't all that excited. I'd always been interested in polenta and grits, whereas mush sounded like some kind of backwoods mountain food. And the sad reality is that if you were to make mush with most any commercial cornmeal on the market, you wouldn't think it was much (or is that "mush"?) either.

If you aren't familiar with the name, mush is an old American dish that's basically just plain-and-simple cooked cornmeal porridge. It's pronounced like "rush," not "push." Pretty much anything you do with grits or polenta you can do with mush. Which is why the first question that most everyone who doesn't know the dish asks, "What's the difference between mush, polenta and grits?"

And a fine question it is. In a broad sense you can certainly stick all three into the same category—porridge made of dried ground corn. Taking the level of detail down a bit, grits tend to be the most coarsely ground, polenta is ground more finely, and cornmeal for traditional mush is finer still. (There are of course exceptions, which is . . . fine.) While the casual cook might think that they sound like pretty much the same thing by different names, in the American South grits and mush are very definitely different. And for reasons I don't yet fully understand, grits are more or less unknown in the culinary traditions north of the Mason-Dixon line, while mush is all over old New England as well as Southern cooking.

I can't really recall why one day I set out to make mush. Blessedly, the first time I did it I used some of the most amazing cornmeal available and topped it with some of the best bacon and bacon fat (Benton's, actually) you can find. Given how I preach about the power of superior ingredients I shouldn't have been so shocked at how good it was. I made mush five more times in the next two weeks, and I've continued to cook it regularly whenever I've got the time. There's really no work to it—you just have to get up and stir every 15 minutes or so (or, alternatively, use a non-stick pot).

Let me emphasize that this recipe, then, isn't really just about making mush for its own sake. Since the ingredients are really just cornmeal, water and salt it's only going to be as good as the corn that goes into it: do it with sit-on-the-shelf, super-processed, "germless" Quaker cornmeal and it's going to be about as exciting as white toast with bad butter. This here dish—as you might have noticed from its well-branded title—is all about *mush made from Anson Mills cornmeal.* The bacon is great on top, but without great cornmeal it's like putting an outstanding olive oil atop so-so pasta. You need the two in concert for the dish to work.

Almost anything goes with mush—certainly most any sautéed or roasted vegetable would be good. But what I've been making at home is a dish from the Civil War era—just mush served up with fried bacon pieces and a lot of bacon fat. Which bacon you use is really up to you since it's so simple and so much the featured flavor along with that of the corn.

Ingredients:

4 cups water
1 cup Anson Mills stone-ground organic yellow cornmeal
1 teaspoon coarse sea salt, plus more to taste
4 ounces sliced bacon (about 2 to 3 slices), chopped
Freshly ground Tellicherry black pepper to taste

Procedure:

Put the water in a heavy stockpot and warm it over medium heat. When the water approaches the boiling point, start adding the cornmeal a bit at a time, stirring to keep the consistency smooth. Add the salt and continue to stir well. Bring the mixture to a light boil and cook, stirring regularly, for a few minutes until the water and meal are well combined. Reduce the heat to very low, cover and cook for as many hours as you can. Simply lift the cover and stir gently 3 or 4 times an hour. If you can keep the heat low enough and you're around the house anyways, there's no reason not to cook it for a good 2 to 4 hours. The longer you let the cooking go with a great fresh cornmeal like Anson Mills, the better it's going to taste.

When you're ready to serve, put the bacon into a hot skillet and cook it until lightly browned. When the bacon's almost done, put the mush into warm serving bowls. Pour the bacon and fat over the top, pass the salt and pepper and enjoy!

Serves 2 to 4 as a main course, depending on how hungry you are, or 6 to 8 as a side dish

FOUR OTHER WAYS TO
MAKE MUSH WITH BACON

There are really only two reasons I can think of not to make mush: not being able to get good cornmeal, and not having time to cook it. So once you've decided to make it, I say you might as well cook a lot of it. It takes no longer to stir a double batch than a single one. It keeps well, too, so you can reheat at will. And there are actually a whole mess of different ways to serve mush other than just eating it on its own. Here's a series of options to consider.

Option 1: With oysters

Just before the bacon is done, add a mess of shucked oysters to the skillet—anywhere from 4 to 14 per person, depending on how flush (and hungry) you're feeling.

Option 2: With fried egg

Just lay it atop everything else. It's a great alternative to the classic bacon, grits and eggs.

Option 3: Fried mush

So much of this book is about fried bacon, but mush is often served that way, as well—cooked, cooled and then cut into slabs and fried up the next day. Bacon fat, sprinkles of crisp bacon and maybe some grated cheddar would be the obvious Southern choices. But you could certainly top yours with butter or olive oil, instead. I like to serve fried mush atop fresh spinach that has been sautéed, as it should be, in bacon fat. Or try caramelized Vidalia or other sweet onions.

Option 4: Sweet mush

You can serve this for breakfast or dessert, topped with maple or sorghum syrup. It's delicious any time of day.

Up in New England, sweet mush is commonly known as "hasty pudding." It seems to be a precursor of Indian pudding, which required more ingredients and started to get closer to the steamed puddings the colonists craved from back home in Britain. In New England, hasty pudding is often (though not always) eaten with a sweet topping, such as maple syrup. This is fine, but I swear by the Southern version, which is topped with sorghum syrup. The official line from Anson Mills' Glenn Roberts on the subject is: "Yummy." "My daughter Ansley would fight for this dish," he says, "and she's a pacifist."

The sweetness and corniness of the corn come up against the slightly sour, just a bit bitter, deep dark sweetness of the sorghum. (Glenn suggested the term "whiplash" to describe this sweet/sour phenomenon, just as it was used to describe the best Madeira back in Colonial times.)

Mush would be good with molasses too, I'm sure. And any of the syrup options is good with a bit of fried bacon thrown on top, of course . . .

Cornmeal Cush

The name is likely a contraction of "cornmeal" and "mush," and the dish is simple but delicious. It's an old-time Southern approach to cornmeal that's just a slight twist on the basic recipe for mush, but will get you a more bacon-y bowl of goodness.

Ingredients:

4 ounces sliced bacon (about 2 to 3 slices), chopped
2 ounces bacon, in a single chunk
4 cups water
1 teaspoon coarse sea salt, plus more to taste
1 cup Anson Mills stone-ground cornmeal (or any other really good cornmeal you care to use)
Freshly ground Tellicherry black pepper to taste

Procedure:

Fry both the chopped and chunk bacon in a heavy 6-quart stockpot until the chopped bacon is done and the chunk is crisp on the outside.

Meanwhile, bring the water to a boil in a medium-sized saucepan and add a teaspoon or so of salt.

When the bacon is done, remove it and reduce the heat to medium low. Add the cornmeal to the bacon fat, stirring steadily so it doesn't burn or stick. Cook over low heat for about 5 minutes. Add a bit of the water and stir immediately to make a paste. Add more water, stirring until well blended with the cornmeal. Continue until all the water has been added. Bring to a slight boil, stir well, and turn heat to low.

Add the bacon chunk back into the pan, stir again and cover. Cook the cush for at least an hour, stirring occasionally to keep it from sticking. When you're ready to serve, remove the bacon chunk from the pot. Chop it into small pieces and heat it along with the reserved bacon pieces in a skillet until crisp.

Spoon the cush into warm bowls, pour the bacon and bacon fat over the top and serve with salt and pepper.

Serves 2 to 4 as a main course, or 6 to 8 as a side dish

Irish Bacon and Cabbage

As you've already learned, in Ireland it's far more typical to cook bacon with cabbage than corned beef. I'd serve the dish with a little mustard and parsley sauce and maybe some hot mashed potatoes.

Ingredients:

FOR THE BACON AND CABBAGE

    2 pounds Irish bacon (brined pork loin, *not smoked*), in a single chunk
    1 carrot, roughly chopped
    2 stalks celery, thickly sliced
    2 leeks, washed well and sliced
    1 medium onion, roughly chopped
    2 teaspoons fresh thyme
    1 tablespoon whole Tellicherry black peppercorns
    1 large head green cabbage, core removed, cut into 6 pieces
    Coarse sea salt to taste
    Freshly ground Tellicherry black pepper to taste

FOR MUSTARD AND PARSLEY SAUCES

    4 tablespoons unsalted butter
    2 tablespoons flour
    ¾ cup bacon stock (reserved from cooking the bacon)

¾ cup whole milk
1 tablespoon brown mustard
¼ cup parsley, finely chopped, rinsed and squeezed dry
Coarse sea salt to taste
Freshly ground Tellicherry black pepper to taste

Procedure:

Place bacon in a large stockpot and fill with cold water to cover. Bring to a rapid boil, then immediately drain and rinse. Return the bacon to the pot with fresh cold water to cover again. Place on high heat, adding the carrot, celery, leeks, onion, thyme and peppercorns. Add more water if needed to just cover the bacon and vegetables. Bring to a boil, then reduce to a simmer. Cover pan loosely, allowing steam to escape, and cook for 1½ to 2 hours. The bacon should be fork tender.

Remove the bacon from the pot and set aside. Strain the stock and set it aside. Discard the cooked vegetables and return the stock to the pot, reserving the ¾ cup for making the mustard and parsley sauces. Return the bacon to the pot. Add the cabbage, placing the pieces around the sides. Cook over medium-high heat for 20 minutes, until cabbage is tender. Add salt and pepper to taste.

While the cabbage is cooking, prepare the mustard and parsley sauces:

Melt the butter in a small saucepan over medium-high heat. Sift flour directly into the butter, whisking constantly until the sauce thickens and a roux forms, 2 to 3 minutes. Slowly add the reserved stock, a bit at a time, whisking with each addition until thickened. Add milk a little at a time, stirring steadily, until incorporated. Split the resulting béchamel evenly into two serving bowls. Whisk the parsley into one bowl and the mustard into the other. Add salt and pepper to taste.

When the cabbage is tender and the sauces are ready to serve, remove the bacon from the pot. Cut into medium-thick slices. Ladle the cabbage into warm serving bowls along with the sliced bacon.

Serves 4 as a main course

Lex's Roast Chicken with Bacon and Spicy Coffee Spice Rub

My friend Lex Alexander turned me on to this recipe about 10 years ago. It's in *Zingerman's Guide to Good Eating* and has become one of the staples of our catering work here at Zingerman's. I loved it from day one because it's such a nice way to make a mini-Thanksgiving dinner without having to spend two days cooking: the chicken juices drip down on the bread beneath it in the roasting dish, essentially creating a low-labor but high-flavor version of stuffing (which I love!). In working on this book it dawned on me that getting bacon involved in the dish would be a big win. So here it is, Lex's chicken take two . . . this time with bacon.

I also decided to add a spice rub that Roadhouse chef and managing partner Alex Young did for *Esquire* magazine a few years ago. Zingerman's Spicy Coffee Spice Rub is a blend of ground Roadhouse Joe coffee, Urfa red pepper from Turkey, Tellicherry black pepper, cloves and sea salt. I really like the coffee, clove and bacon blend of flavors—in some strange way it makes me think about a spicy, exotic version of red eye gravy. It's appropriate, too, since Lex's current life revolves a lot around the very fine coffee shop—called 3 Cups—he owns in Chapel Hill, NC. Having tried the dish with a number of different bacons, we settled on Allan Benton's—its big smoky favor and silky fat served the dish well!

It should probably go without saying, but the better the chicken, the better the dish. I use free-range birds we buy from Amish farmers in Indiana. The chicken smells great in the oven, too—the aromas of roasting chicken and bacon both make me want to eat as soon as the thing starts cooking.

Ingredients:

- 1¼ pounds sliced Benton's bacon (about 12 slices)
- 2 large Spanish onions (about 1½ pounds), cut in half lengthwise and sliced into thin half circles
- 4 stalks celery, cut into ⅛-inch slices
- 1¼ pounds tart apples (about 3 medium), ½-inch dice, skins on
- 1 scant cup dried currants
- 1 clove fresh garlic, minced
- ½ teaspoon dried thyme or 1 tablespoon fresh thyme
- 1 teaspoon hot red pepper flakes (preferably Marash)

1 tablespoon lemon zest

1 teaspoon coarse sea salt

2 teaspoons freshly ground Tellicherry black pepper

¼ cup parsley, chopped, rinsed and squeezed dry

½ loaf leftover country bread, such as a good crusty white country loaf, sliced ¾-inch thick. If the bread is still fresh and soft, slice it and let it dry on the counter for a few hours before using.

1 roasting chicken (3 to 4 pounds), split in half and backbone removed

5 tablespoons Zingerman's Spicy Coffee Spice Rub (or you can make your own—the ingredients are listed above)

¼ cup fresh-squeezed lemon juice

Procedure:

Preheat oven to 400°F

Arrange 6 of the bacon slices on a ½-inch-deep baking sheet. Bake for 20 minutes, or until the bacon is crisp and most of its fat is rendered. Remove the baking sheet carefully from the oven. Drain bacon on paper towels and reserve for another use. When the fat cools a bit, pour into a Pyrex measuring cup. You should have about ½ cup.

Heat ¼ cup of the fat in a large skillet over low heat. Add the onion and celery. Cover and sweat, stirring occasionally, for 15 minutes or until soft.

Add the apple, currants, garlic, thyme, red pepper flakes, lemon zest, salt and black pepper. Stir to mix. Cook, covered, until the onions and celery are translucent, about 5 to 7 more minutes. Remove from heat, stir in the parsley, and set aside.

Lightly brush the bottom and sides of a 15-inch oval roasting pan with 1 tablespoon of the rendered bacon fat. Arrange the bread slices to cover the entire bottom of the baking dish. (If the bread is too big to fit easily, simply cut the slices into smaller pieces so that they tile the entire bottom of the dish properly.)

Layer the onion mixture atop the bread. Place the chicken, skin side up, over the onion mixture and bread. Rub it with 2 tablespoons of bacon fat and 4 tablespoons of Coffee Spice Rub. Pour the lemon juice over the chicken, then lay the remaining bacon slices across the top of the chicken.

Place the entire dish in the oven and cook, uncovered. After 45 minutes or so, check that the bacon has crisped on top of the chicken. Once it has, pull it off the chicken and lay it directly onto the bread mixture so the chicken can brown. Change the oven function to broil, but continue at

400°F. The chicken should be done in 15 to 20 minutes: the skin should be nicely crisped and its juices should run clear when the bird is pricked with a fork.

Remove the pan from the oven. Sprinkle the whole dish with 1 tablespoon Coffee Spice Rub and let stand for a few minutes. Remove the chicken to a cutting board and cut into quarters. Draw a sharp knife through the bacon, bread and onion mixture to break it up. Spoon some of the mixture onto each plate and place the chicken on top.

Serves 4 as a main course

Pasta alla Gricia

The background on this dish is provided in the section on guanciale (see page 118), so all I'll say here is that it's a really great bowl of pasta, and that the pepper is one of the key components of this dish, not a postscript, so use a lot of it.

The more I eat this dish, the more I like it.

Ingredients:

1 pound spaghetti (I'm partial to Martelli, but you can pick from any of the great artisan brands including Latini, Rustichella and Cavalieri)
5 ounces (about 2 to 3 slices) guanciale, diced
Hot red pepper flakes (preferably Marash), to taste
Freshly ground Tellicherry black pepper to taste
5 ounces Italian Pecorino Romano cheese, finely grated

Procedure:

Bring a large pot of water to a boil. Add a generous amount of salt.

At the same time, begin heating a heavy 12-inch skillet over medium-high heat.

Add the pasta to the water and stir so that the noodles don't stick.

Fry the guanciale in the skillet until its fat is released and the nuggets begin to crisp. (If your guanciale is too lean, add a bit of olive oil to the pan.)

When the pasta is approaching but not quite yet *al dente*, remove from the heat and drain.

Add the pasta to the skillet with the guanciale and toss well to coat with the hot pork fat. Cook over medium heat for about 2 minutes, until the pasta is fully *al dente*. Stir regularly so that the pasta doesn't stick. Add red pepper flakes and black pepper liberally to taste.

Turn off the heat, add the grated Pecorino cheese and toss to coat. Serve hot, and pass the pepper grinder.

Variation:

In the spring, sauté 6 ounces of asparagus, cut into 1-inch pieces, along with the guanciale. I like the asparagus pieces lightly browned to bring out their full flavor.

Serves 4 as a main course, or 6 to 8 as a side dish

Spaghetti alla Carbonara

If you want to cook pancetta instead of eating it raw, it's really good for making pasta carbonara. (Guanciale would also be great—it's a bit richer, pancetta a bit more seasoned.) Regardless of which pork you pick, carbonara in Italy is usually a far yellower looking dish than it usually is here. Because eggs are such a big part of the recipe, the radically richer colors of Italian egg yolks (the difference is the feed) might make you think there's saffron in the sauce. Fortunately, as egg quality improves here in the States you've got a better chance of replicating that richness of both color and flavor.

This recipe is from the Martelli family in Tuscany, who makes some of the best pasta I've ever had. Their maccheroni is one of the very few non-American ingredients we feature at the Roadhouse—it's just so much better than any other macaroni that I can't stand not to serve it.

When you get to the saucing steps at the end of the recipe it's important to move very quickly. Clear the decks so you can move from pot to plate without any obstacles—you don't want to overcook the egg and lose the heat of the dish.

This recipe calls for spaghetti, but the truth is I've had good carbonara with other shapes, too. Also, I know that in Rome it would be more typical to use Pecorino Romano than Parmigiano, but since this came from the

Martellis up in Tuscany and they, like most of their neighbors, use Parmigiano, I've stuck with that here. The truth is, either is quite good!

Ingredients:

1 pound Martelli spaghetti
6 ounces (about 3 slices) pancetta (or guanciale), diced
1 tablespoon extra virgin olive oil
6 fresh eggs, beaten
2 ounces Parmigiano-Reggiano, or more to taste
Coarse sea salt to taste
Freshly ground Tellicherry black pepper to taste

Procedure:

Bring a large pot of salted water to a boil and add the spaghetti. Stir well to keep from sticking. Cook until *al dente*, about 10 minutes or so.

Meanwhile, in a 12-inch skillet fry the pancetta in the olive oil until the fat is completely melted and the meat is crisp. Remove the pancetta from the pan, reserving the fat. Reduce the heat to low, being careful not to burn the fat.

When the spaghetti is done, drain and toss with the fat in the skillet.

Working quickly, pour the eggs over the pasta. Don't dally or the mix will get cold; at the same time you don't want the pan too hot, lest the eggs overcook. Quickly add the pancetta, lots of freshly ground pepper, stir well and get it out of the skillet and into very warm bowls ASAP. Salt to taste, then sprinkle some freshly grated Parmigiano-Reggiano over the top, and eat it while it's hot!

Serves 4 as a main course, or 6 to 8 as a side dish

Shrimp and Grits with Benton's Bacon

I first had shrimp and grits down in South Carolina, where it's as standard a feature of the cuisine as clam chowder would be in New England. Unfortunately, people who've never had this dish almost always look at me a bit oddly when I mention it. Northerners—who often know little or nothing about grits in the first place—get even more anxious when you start talking to them about putting what they think is some tasteless amorphous, pasty white porridge (that being the "grits") next to their beloved shrimp. Of course, most Americans have never had great grits. Fewer still have ever experienced really good, fresh shrimp. But when you do the dish right— with really good grits and fresh in-the-shell shrimp—it's one of the best things I've ever had for brunch. As always, I love the Anson Mills white grits that we use here at Zingerman's. And because I want to bring the bacon flavor fully up front, I like this dish with Benton's or Edwards' dry-cured offerings.

If you're interested in other good versions of this dish, check out *Nathalie Dupree's Shrimp and Grits Cookbook*.

Note that you'll need some cheesecloth to tie up the shrimp shells for cooking into the sauce.

Ingredients:

FOR THE GRITS:

4 cups water
1 cup coarse-ground grits
¾ teaspoon coarse sea salt
2 tablespoons butter

FOR THE SHRIMP SAUCE:

4 ounces (about 2 to 3 slices) bacon, diced
12 fresh shell-on jumbo shrimp
½ teaspoon coarse sea salt, plus additional to taste
½ stalk celery, coarsely chopped
1 small sweet onion, coarsely chopped
1 large red bell pepper, coarsely chopped
1 clove fresh garlic, chopped fine
1 tablespoon flour

2 cups water
2 bay leaves
Hot red pepper flakes (preferably Marash), to taste
Freshly ground Tellicherry black pepper to taste

Procedure:

Heat the water in a large pot over high heat. Add the grits before it begins to boil, stirring well. Continue stirring while the pot comes to a boil, then reduce the heat. Add the salt and butter, stirring for a minute to melt the butter. Hold the pot at a low boil, stirring the grits regularly until they begin to thicken (3 to 5 minutes).

Reduce the heat to medium-low and simmer, loosely covered, for 30 to 60 minutes—or longer still—until grits reach desired doneness. The longer you cook 'em, the better they'll get. Stir fairly often to avoid clumping and sticking.

While the grits are cooking, start the sauce.

Cook the bacon in a 13-inch skillet over medium heat for a few minutes until lightly cooked and the fat is rendered. Remove half the bacon from the pan and reserve, leaving the other half in the skillet with the fat.

Add the shrimp to the skillet, sprinkle with salt and sauté briefly so that they're very lightly cooked—but not cooked through—on each side (probably less than a minute per side). Remove shrimp to a platter and set aside.

In the same skillet, sauté the onion, celery, red bell pepper, and garlic until the vegetables are soft and lightly browned, 10 to 12 minutes. Meanwhile, shell and clean the shrimp, reserving the shells and tying them in a cheesecloth bundle.

Sift the flour directly over the vegetables and give it a good stir until it dissolves. Slowly add in the water, mixing constantly, so that it forms a smooth sauce. Bring the mixture to a high simmer and cook for a couple of minutes, stirring steadily.

Add the shrimp shell bundle, the bay leaves, reserved bacon and red pepper flakes. Keep at a low simmer for 15 to 30 minutes or until the grits (which are cooking in the other pot) are almost ready. Add additional water if the sauce gets too thick. It should be the texture of a moderately thick pasta sauce.

Cut the peeled and cleaned shrimp into 1-inch pieces. (You can leave them whole if your prefer, but I like the more effective shrimp distribution that you get from having smaller pieces.) Return to the sauce and simmer for a few more minutes. Remove and discard the shells. Add salt and pepper to taste.

Ladle the cooked grits onto warm plates. Top with the shrimp sauce, sprinkle on the reserved fried bacon and serve hot.

Serves 3 to 4 as a main course

Wittenberg Splits

This is the way Tanya Nueske and her family grew up eating hot dogs. They're not hard to make and they really are darned good. To restate the by-now familiar: the better the buns and hot dogs, the better these are going to taste. I use buns from Zingerman's Bakehouse, on which I put either Vienna all-beef dogs from Chicago (the ones I grew up with) or the Niman Ranch version. Take note that in Wisconsin "cheddar" *always* means orange cheese, never white. It won't taste any different, but if you want to accurately replicate Tanya Nueske's early life experience, white cheese just really won't do.

Ingredients:

12 thick slices Nueske's applewood-smoked bacon
6 jumbo hot dogs, split lengthwise
6 ounces sharp cheddar (the older the better), sliced
1 large dill pickle, sliced thinly lengthwise
6 hot dog buns, toasted

Procedure:

Preheat oven to broil at 375°F.

With a sharp paring knife, cut a line lengthwise along each hot dog, leaving a thin strip at the bottom so that the dog stays in one piece. Lay the sliced cheddar inside the split, then place a long slice of pickle atop the cheese. Wrap each hot dog in 2 slices of bacon and secure the ends of each strip with a toothpick.

Place on a foil-topped baking sheet and broil for 10 to 12 minutes, or until the bacon is nicely browned.

You can put your buns under the broiler for the last 2 minutes to toast them, too. Take out the toothpicks, put the dogs in the buns and eat 'em while they're hot.

Serves 6 as a main course

TLBBLT:
The Laurel Blakemore
Bacon, Lettuce and Tomato Sandwich

Aside from being the only palindromic recipe name I know, this also makes a really good sandwich, which has long been very popular at the Deli. It's named for Dr. Laurel Blakemore, horse fanatic, show jumper, pediatric orthopaedic surgeon and a big lover of bacon. It calls for a good bit of mayonnaise—I think a good BLT needs that, but you can certainly cut back if you like. Either way, it's easy to make and great to eat!

The recipe is for a single sandwich but it's not hard to do the math and make as many as you want.

Ingredients:

2 to 4 slices Arkansas peppered bacon
2 slices crusty country bread (we use Zingerman's Farm Bread)
2 tablespoons mayonnaise
2 slices aged Vermont cheddar cheese
2 thick slices good tomato
Handful of good lettuce

Procedure:

Cook the bacon in a frying pan until done. Remove from pan and drain, but leave the pan on the heat.

Spread mayonnaise on both slices of bread. Put a slice of cheese on each slice, then add the bacon and tomato. Assemble the sandwich, give it a gentle press together with your palm and slide it into the hot pan. Weight it down with a bowl and fry until golden brown. Flip, brown the other side, and remove from pan. Add the lettuce, cut the sandwich on whatever angle your heart desires (remember, though, that Laurel is a surgeon and places great value on properly positioned knife cuts!), and eat it while it's hot!

Bacon and Burgers:
A "Best of" List

Bacon and burgers are such a great combination, enhanced even further by a bit of cheese on top of it all. I'm burger-blessed here at Zingerman's because we use only fresh chuck from Niman Ranch (there are other good sources, of course; but theirs has been consistently good) that we grind every day and then grill over oak.

There's no end to the combinations, but here's a list to get you started:

BLUE CHEESE AND BACON BURGER

When I eat blue cheese on its own I tend to like the bigger, smokier, rootsier options like Stilton and Roquefort. But with a burger I lean toward the sweeter side, with blues like Iowa Maytag and its very well-made, nicely nuanced progeny—Point Reyes Blue—from the Giacomini family north of San Francisco.

PIMENTO CHEESE AND ARKANSAS PEPPERED BACON BURGER

My favorite at the Roadhouse. You'll find our pimento cheese recipe in this book—it has become a Zingerman's classic. I would respectfully say that we really do seem to be making Ann Arbor the pimento cheese capital of the Midwest (with all due deference to the South, of course, where this delicious cheese dip originated). The good ingredients we use to make our pimento cheese into something really exceptionally, ethereally, energetically good on its own make it equally exceptional on a burger. We have many customers who now eat one of these on almost every visit. If you're making it at home, a great way is to stuff the cheese into the burgers before cooking (thanks to Molly Stevens for that suggestion). It makes for a great eating experience—the slight crispiness of the burger's "crust" from the grill, the tenderness of the ground beef, and then the oozy spiciness of the cheese at the heart of it all. It's best topped with good bacon—I'm partial to the Arkansas peppered variety myself.

BACON AND EGG BURGER

The burger of choice for the bacon 'n' eggs crowd. I'd go with Edwards'
(my favorite bacon with eggs) and a really good egg over easy atop a
burger on a toasted bun.

24/7 BURGER

This is a burger we've been doing at the Roadhouse for a while now, and
it's got quite the loyal following. It's all about Wisconsin and big flavors
with a touch of natural sweetness: we do it with the smoked for 24 hours
over applewood bacon from Nueske's and the aged for seven years cheddar from Tony and Julie Hook in Mineral Point, Wisconsin . . . hence the
name.

JIFFY BURGER

Joeli Yaguda is not the person from whom I'd have expected to learn
about Jiffy Burgers. She grew up in California and produces some of this
country's best olive oil. While she does like bacon with a passion, a burger
with bacon and peanut butter and Nebraska (or Missouri, depending on
who you talk to) roots doesn't really seem like it'd be up her culinary alley.
But she swore by the concept so ardently one night that I had to check it
out. I don't really like peanut butter and even if I did the idea of peanut
butter and bacon on a burger would make me cringe. "You have to try it,"
she said. "It's incredible." Judith and Evan Jones do have a peanut butter
and bacon muffin in the classic *Book of Bread,* and of course Elvis used to
eat bacon, peanut butter and banana sandwiches. On top of which, I guess
there's something spiritually complete about the idea of peanut-fed pigs
being made into bacon which is then eaten with peanut butter. So there
you have it.

There are I'm sure a thousand other bacon and burger combinations
worth considering. I'd be very glad to hear about your favorites—feel free
to email away to baconbits@zingermans.com.

Kentucky Green Beans with Bacon

If you serve lightly cooked green beans to a courteous Kentuckian, they'll probably just politely pick at 'em for a bit before leaving the rest on the plate uneaten. A more forceful compatriot (like maybe Daniel Boone, if he should happen in for dinner) wouldn't be so subtle—they'd quickly call on you to put the beans back into the pot for at least a couple of hours longer. To get the point across, I'll just say that quick-cook green beans are as unacceptable to most Kentucky country folk as turkey bacon would be at Allan Benton's breakfast table. Green beans in the Bluegrass state are not an *al dente* dish!

Basically, this is the same sort of recipe you'd expect to find if you were cooking up a mess of long-cooked collards. One key is to use mature pole beans (not standard green beans)—they can absorb a lot more of the liquid and hence are more flavorful when they're finished. For the pork, I prefer to use the Finchville Farms unsmoked, dry-cured bacon, because that's what Bill Robertson reminded me over and over again it was made for. (Although Bill was really adamant, I won't yell at you if you use one of the other good-quality smoked bacons—the beans will be good, regardless.)

The main point is that since all that's in here is the bacon and the green beans you don't really want to skimp on the quality of either. During the long cooking the fat from the bacon penetrates into the beans and makes for a pretty rich dish. I don't actually get the science of it, but the two rounds of boiling for the beans (two hours, then drain, then do it again with the bacon in the pot) seem to make a big difference.

These beans are generally used as a side dish, but there's no reason they can't be a main course for baco-tarians, or even just for folks like me who like to eat a lot of vegetables.

Ingredients:

2 pounds fresh green pole beans or broad beans, strings removed and broken into 3-inch pieces
6 ounces Finchville Farms unsmoked country-cured bacon, in a single chunk
1 tablespoon coarse sea salt
Freshly ground Tellicherry black pepper to taste

Procedure:

Bring a large pot of salted water to a boil. Add the beans and simmer for 2 hours, or until the beans are fork tender. Drain and rinse. (This removes the starch from the mature beans. Note: If you're using tender bush green beans, you can skip this first step entirely.)

Return the beans to the pot and add the bacon and water just to cover. Cook over medium-low heat for 2 more hours, until the bacon has rendered its fat and the water has reduced to just a little bit of savory broth.

Remove the bacon, chop it coarsely and add it back into the beans. Add salt and pepper to taste.

Serves 6 to 8 as a side dish

Cheddar Bacon Scones

A variation on the cheddar herb scones that we've long made at Zingerman's Bakehouse, these aren't hard to make and they're pretty delicious. Paul Saginaw (with whom I started the Deli back in 1982) took home the whole platter of them after we did the first test!

I prefer to use cultured butter because it's got a bigger flavor, and if you want to eat extravagantly you can gild the lily by serving them with room-temperature butter for spreading when they come warm from the oven. Very rich and really, really good.

Ingredients:

8 ounces sliced Arkansas peppered bacon (about 4 to 6 slices)
2½ cups all-purpose flour
4 teaspoons baking powder
½ teaspoon fine sea salt
¾ cup unsalted butter, cut into ½-inch pieces, cold
2 large eggs, beaten, cold
½ cup plus 2 tablespoons heavy cream, cold
4 ounces Vermont cheddar (at least 1 year old, 2 is even better), crumbled and cold
3 scallions, chopped

Procedure:

Fry the bacon over medium heat until crisp. Drain, chop and place in refrigerator to cool.

Preheat oven to 375°F.

Sift the flour, baking powder and salt into a large mixing bowl. Cut in the butter with a knife or pastry cutter until the mixture forms ½-inch pieces.

Add the eggs, ½ cup of the cream, and cheddar. Mix by hand until just combined. Fold in scallions.

Transfer the dough to a well-floured board. Form two 7-inch rounds. Cut each into 6 wedges.

Transfer the wedges to a baking sheet lined with parchment. Brush with the remaining cream and bake for 20 to 25 minutes, until the scones are golden brown on the top and bottom (you'll have to lift them off the baking sheet a bit to check underneath).

Allow to cool and firm up for about 10 minutes before removing from sheet. Serve the same day.

Makes 12 small scones

Apple (or Pear) Bacon Crisp

S trange as it sounds to some, bacon really can beget a fine dessert. As someone at the Roadhouse said when we had this on our dessert list a while back, "You might think bacon and apples sounds strange for dessert, but it's basically like serving pork chops with applesauce." Made sense to me. And for folks who love their bacon, it's a very good way to get a bit more into their day.

The crisp is a great autumn dessert and would be excellent for both eating and engaging guests in conversation at holiday meals. You can do it with pears instead of apples, with equally good results. In truth, I almost like it better that way, but they're both darned good! Take your pick, or, if you're entertaining, do one of each and let your guests decide.

Ingredients:

> ¾ cup golden raisins
> 3 tablespoons bourbon
> 6 ounces sliced Arkansas peppered or long pepper bacon (about 3 to 4 slices), diced

¾ cup Muscovado (or other natural dark) brown sugar
9 to 12 ripe apples or pears (about 2½ pounds)
1¼ teaspoons cinnamon
¼ cup unsalted butter

FOR THE STREUSEL:

½ cup unsalted butter, chilled and cut into ½-inch pieces
1¼ cups flour
¼ cup Muscovado (or other natural dark) brown sugar
¼ cup sugar
¼ teaspoon fine sea salt

Procedure:

Preheat oven to 400°F.

Pour the bourbon over the raisins, mix well and set aside to soak for a minimum of 15 minutes, on up to a couple of hours (longer is better to my taste, but if you forget to do it ahead the shorter time will work just fine).

Dredge the bacon in ¾ cup of brown sugar and lay on a foil-lined baking sheet with a lip. Sprinkle any of the remaining brown sugar over the top. Bake for 20 minutes or until very dark brown, crisp and caramelized. Carefully remove from oven and allow to cool.

While bacon is cooking, slice the fruit (skin on) directly into a 9-inch round pan. After you've covered the bottom of the pan, sprinkle on some of the raisins, then a bit of the bourbon and the cinnamon. Add another layer of fruit, then the remaining raisins and cinnamon. Sprinkle the balance of the bourbon over the top and dot with the butter. (The sliced fruit may pile up over the lip of the pan, but it will settle while baking.) Sprinkle the candied bacon pieces evenly over the top.

Reduce the oven temperature to 375°F.

Make the streusel by combining the butter, flour, salt and sugars in a mixer or food processor. The mixture should be crumbly and somewhat dry. Sprinkle over the top of the apple mixture in the pan and pat down lightly. Go around the edges, pressing the streusel into the fruit to seal.

Place the dish in the oven uncovered and bake for 30 to 40 minutes, until the juices are bubbling up around the edges and the streusel is nicely browned. Remove from the oven and cool for 15 minutes.

Serve warm, with optional ice cream or gelato.

Serves 6 to 8 for dessert

Chocolate and Bacon Fat Gravy

When I first read about this recipe I thought it was probably some-where between a bad fad and a silly joke about Southern folk. I knew about chicken gravy, beef gravy, red eye gravy, even Wavy Gravy, but chocolate gravy made with bacon fat certainly wasn't found in the dining car of any gravy train I'd been riding on. Me and 99.7 percent of my fellow Americans are probably in the same (gravy) boat on this one—most every-one whom I mention this to thinks I'm messing with them. A few do get excited, but they're mostly folks who want to feel like they're out in front of the trends and get all wired up about the creative ways they're going to work chocolate gravy into their everyday eating routines. But as silly or stupendous as the dish sounds to you, chocolate gravy is neither a joke nor a new Ferran Adria-inspired deconstruction. It's the real thing—a recipe with roots, and, appropriately for me, a bit of a strange and fascinating his-tory. Most importantly, it actually tastes great.

I first got wind of chocolate gravy from John T. Edge and Angie Mosier of the Southern Foodways Alliance. The recipe below is adapted from one they sent me, inspired by Mrs. Sue Herring of Saltillo, Mississippi. I received another inspirational recipe from the aptly named Fred Sauce-man, a professor of Appalachian Studies at East Tennessee State, who has got as much passion for Appalachian authenticity as anyone I've ever met. Check out his series, "The Place Setting," and in particular the essay enti-tled "The Randomness of Chocolate Gravy."

Assuming that you're not of Appalachian origin and don't study this obscure foodways stuff as obsessively as folks like Fred Sauceman and I do, it would be a pretty natural thing to won-der what the heck chocolate gravy really is and where it comes from. It would be reasonable to assume that its ori-gins lie with some modern-day Edward Bernays—that cheerleader of bacon and eggs. If you wanted to sell a product, the concept of pre-packaged chocolate gravy seems almost too good to be true. But, as I said above, there are no marketing machinations at work here; this stuff is for real and is authentically Appalachian.

How Appalachians got started eating it, I can't say for sure; the dish's
exact origins remain murky. Fred Sauceman shared several theories. It
could have some connection to traditional Mexican moles, which, of
course, also mix cacao with savory and sweet into a sauce of this sort. Or
perhaps it came up from the Spanish colonies on the East Coast. Fred's
theory, which makes good sense to me, is that when an affordable Hershey's cocoa came to the hills in the twentieth century, people added it to
the gravy they were already making all the time anyways, thus adding sweetness and richness to lives that were not exactly replete with either (at least
in a material, if not necessarily an emotional, sense). I can see chocolate
gravy as a serious Sunday treat for poor kids in the hills or for most of the
folks you'll find in Harriette Arnow's novels about rural Kentucky.

It was also Fred Sauceman who taught me about the connection
between chocolate gravy and the Melungeons—and here we're getting way
deep into the obscure stuff. Chocolate gravy might be an odd-sounding
dish, but the Melungeons make it look like a hit TV show. Even spell-check
doesn't recognize them, and I'm starting to think that's a more meaningful
measure of modern-day acceptance into American society than the decen-
nial census. Anyway, I hate to digress when I've got you so close to chocolate, but since I've already bored you with sidebars on Hungarian cowboys,
nineteenth-century New England hog-herders, and bacon fat-touting
1950s R&B stars, why not a brief bit on the Melungeons just to muck up
the straightness of this story line? After all, most every cookbook has recipes, but not that many include strange social histories.

The Melungeons—those who eat chocolate gravy and those who
don't—are a group of mixed-race ancestry who have lived primarily in
the hills of Kentucky, Virginia, West Virginia and Tennessee for many
centuries. I learned from Phil Deloria, a good Zingerman's customer and
esteemed professor of Native American history at the University of Michigan, that they're technically what's known as "tri-racial isolates," which
means that they're some part white, some part black and some part Indian.

Theories abound as to their origins—some say they're descendents
of shipwrecked Portuguese, others that their roots lie with a group of
Englishmen who got lost in the mountains and stayed to intermarry with
Indians and early African Americans. Connections to the Cherokees often
come up, as well. It certainly hasn't anything to do with chocolate gravy,
but Melungeon people typically have dark, cocoa-colored skin, often combined with blue eyes. Apparently they referred to themselves throughout

their history as "black Irish," "black Germans" or "black Dutch." As English settlements spread inland from the original colonies nearer the coast, the Melungeons in the southern states were classed as "free colored people," which, while better than being slaves, meant that they weren't allowed to own land, vote, educate their children or marry non-Melungeons. When I read stuff like this . . . I can only shake my head at the mysteries of how human beings work. There were even cases argued before the Tennessee Supreme Court during WWII over whether Melungeons in the military should be classed as "Negroes."

Coming back to the food, the recipe below is a distillation of several that I got from Fred Sauceman and the folks at Southern Foodways. The Melungeons, it seems, are very big on chocolate gravy. Fred was quick to emphasize that the stuff is probably not of Melungeon origin, and others certainly eat it as well. For example, jam-maker April McGreger grew up in Mississippi in non-Melungeon country and says her mother always made the stuff (albeit without the bacon fat you'll find in this version). But according to Fred, chocolate gravy has for some reason found particular favor among Melungeon families.

I'm not Melungeon, nor have I lived in the mountains, but my bias toward darker chocolate and less sweetness got the recipe down to about half the milk it might have had in its original form. Given that it was made up in the mountains, milk, brought in daily from the family cow and hence much less costly than cocoa, might have been the dominant ingredient. I'm not really sure which costs more by the pound anymore, but we're going for flavor first, so a higher ratio of cocoa to milk it is. Same goes for the quality of the cocoa—I use the one we get from Scharffen Berger which is darker than the more out-and-about Hershey's. You can also, of course, simply add more milk or have back at the Hershey's if you're after a mellower flavor.

The main point here, though, isn't chocolate gravy's popularity with Melungeons, but rather that the dish has roots and that it's really good. At its most basic level it may play a role not unlike Nutella for kids across the European continent, or a *pain au chocolat* dipped in a coffee cup for Parisians.

Sara Roahan, who wrote the really good book *Gumbo Tales*, said, "Those southerners really know how to eat. How much happier would my childhood have been with chocolate gravy? I cry to consider the answer." Make chocolate gravy, eat it and weep with joy.

Ingredients:

6 ounces sliced dry-cured smoked bacon (about 3 to 4 slices)(I like the full-
bodied intense flavor of Broadbent's or Benton's)

4 tablespoons bacon fat (rendered from the bacon slices plus any extra fat as
necessary to bring it up to the full measure)

1 cup sugar

¼ cup cocoa powder

3 tablespoons all-purpose flour

1 cup whole milk

Coarse sea salt to taste

Freshly ground Tellicherry black pepper to taste

Procedure:

Fry the bacon in a heavy skillet over medium heat until crisp. Remove and
drain on paper towels. Strain the fat and return 4 tablespoons' worth back
into the skillet. Turn the heat to low.

Combine the sugar, cocoa and flour in a bowl and mix well. Sift into
the hot fat, stirring constantly until blended and the dry ingredients begin
to melt into the bacon fat, about 3 to 4 minutes.

Chop the sliced bacon into small bits and set aside.

Slowly add ¼ cup of the milk to the skillet, stirring constantly. The
mixture will begin to bubble. Turn the heat up a touch and keep stirring
until the sugar mixture is well dissolved. Slowly add the rest of the milk, a
bit at a time, stirring throughout so that the gravy thickens, about 2 to 3
minutes—it should coat the spoon nicely. Add salt and pepper to taste.

Spoon the hot gravy over warm buttered biscuits. (If you're in a pinch
for time and find yourself biscuitless, the gravy is good on white toast, too,
although I don't think that's the mountain man way.) Crumble the bacon
over the top and serve.

Yields about 2 cups, enough to serve 8

TONY SPICER'S EXTRA-SPECIAL TIPS
FOR CHOCOLATE GRAVY

Tony Spicer is one of the folks I've found who was actually raised on chocolate gravy. In his case it was in northeast Arkansas, "right where the Ozarks
meet the Mississippi River Delta lands." I know him because he's married
to Erin Dion, one of the most highly spirited folks in our organization.

When he heard we were starting to make his childhood staple at the Road-house he wrote me a late-night missive on the subject. "I am one of those few, proud Southerners," he said, "who grew up on this stuff. In fact, I attri-bute half the weight of my left leg to the calories provided by this delicacy."

I should tell you that Tony challenged my chocolate gravy chops—which, given that I'm a Jewish kid from Chicago, seems like a very reason-able thing to do. His family has been at this for a while, having emigrated to Arkansas from Tennessee about a century and a half ago. "Brother," he wrote, "you just try to beat my momma's chocolate gravy. I dare ya!" Now I know he was mostly saying that just in jest, but . . . fortunately I'm not a competitive person and I definitely never compete with family recipes and culinary upbringings, leastly when it comes to anything as emotionally complex as chocolate gravy. That said, I think it's easy to imagine family feuds sparked by an implied insult to someone's grandmother's gravy recipe. I stake no claims here to our version being the best—I'm only providing you with a really good way to eat your breakfast this weekend!

Take note that Tony would use only Hershey's cocoa, and for good rea-son since that's what he grew up on. And, as I said, I don't want to be chal-lenging anyone's family recipes. The one provided above is just mine.

Following are a few bonus tips from Tony:

1. Eat your gravy with eggs. "Gotta have 'em, but fried only (scrambled eggs and chocolate gravy turn into a mess)."

2. Have an extra biscuit on the side. Basically, this is a backup. "Chocolate gravy," Tony wrote, "requires an extra biscuit. It just does. The extra biscuit suggests: a) sopping, b) strawberry preserves. Both of these are pretty good ways to cleanse the palate of what will have been a very, very rich meal."

3. Butter the biscuits before you put the gravy on (hard to argue with that one: butter's a close second to bacon in the "Everything's Better With . . . " Olympics).

4. Enjoy some bacon strips with it. "For people who think milk and cookies are the culinary god-food of dipping," Tony told me, "they are wrong. It's a strip of bacon and chocolate gravy."

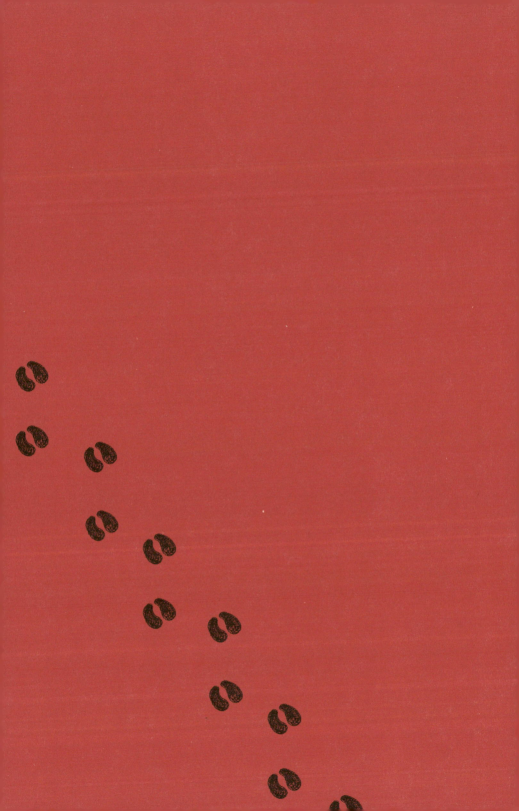

Trivia Test

1. How long ago are wild boars thought to have originated?

2. When were the first pigs brought to North America, and from where?

3. Who was the original Uncle Sam, and what was he famous for?

4. What are the two major styles of curing bacon?

5. What cut do most Americans use for making bacon?

6. And the British?

7. What do British people call American-style belly bacon?

8. Where was the idea of "bringing home the bacon" invented?

9. Where is Burgers' Country Smokehouse located?

10. Along what highway is Allan Benton's smokehouse found?

11. What's a flitch?

12. Name three kinds of heirloom hogs.

13. What kind of wood does each of these bacon makers smoke over:
Sam Edwards, Allan Benton, Tanya Nueske, Steven Burger
and Ron Nodine?

14. About how long does each of these bacon makers smoke for:
Sam Edwards, Allan Benton, Tanya Nueske, Ronny and Beth
Drennan (Broadbent's), Charlie Gatton (Father's),
Ken Haviland (Royal Canadian Bacon Company)?

15. What's the name of the nineteenth-century English bacon cure?

16. Who "invented" the all-American bacon and eggs breakfast?

17. For extra credit, who was his uncle?

18. Name the Appalachian people who particularly enjoy chocolate gravy on their biscuits.

19. What were the men called who walked hogs from farms to the cities for slaughter?

20. In what year did Mr. Bende and his family come to the U.S. from Hungary?

21. In what year did Andre Williams release "Bacon Fat"?

22. In what year did Johnny Cash release "Folsom Prison Blues"?

(Stumped? See the next page for the answers.)

TRIVIA TEST ANSWERS

1. *40,000 years*

2. *In 1539 from Spain with Hernando de Soto*

3. *"Uncle Sam" was 21-year-old Samuel Wilson of New Hampshire. During the War of 1812 he was a pork packer for the Army.*

4. *Wet cure and dry cure*

5. *The belly*

6. *The loin*

7. *Streaky bacon*

8. *Little Dunmow, England*

9. *California, Missouri*

10. *411*

11. *British for a side of bacon*

12. *(Choose any three) Duroc, Lincolnshire Curly Whites, Berkshires, Tamworths, Large Blacks, Middle Whites, Large Whites and Gloucester Old Spots*

13. *Edwards: hickory; Benton: hickory; Nueske: applewood; Burger: hickory; Nodine: apple pomace or juniper*

14. *Edwards: 18–24 hours; Benton: 48 hours; Nueske: 24 hours; Drennan: 2–4 days; Gatton: 48–96 hours; Haviland: Trick question! Canadian bacon is uncured!*

15. *The Wiltshire Cure*

16. *Edward Bernays*

17. *Sigmund Freud*

18. *The Melungeons*

19. *Drovers*

20. *1956*

21. *1956*

22. *1956*

More Bacon Bits

Good Bits of Bacon Information for Your Reading, Researching (and Eating) Pleasure

Bruce Aidells' Complete Book of Pork, by Bruce Aidells (William Morrow, 2004)

Hunter's Horn, by Harriette Simpson Arnow (Macmillan, 1949; reprint Michigan State University Press, 1997)

Seedtime on the Cumberland, by Harriette Simpson Arnow (Macmillan, 1960; reprint Bison Books, 1995)

Flowering of the Cumberland, by Harriette Simpson Arnow (Macmillan, 1963; reprint Bison Books, 1996)

Around the World in 80 Dinners, by Cheryl and Bill Jamison (William Morrow, 2008)

The BLT Cookbook, by Michele Anna Jordan (William Morrow, 2003)

Pig Perfect: Encounters with Remarkable Swine and Some Great Ways to Cook Them, by Peter Kaminsky (Hyperion, 2005)

Early Irish Farming, by Fergus Kelly (Dublin Institute for Advanced Studies, 1988; reprint 2000)

The Cuisine of Hungary, by George Lang (Atheneum, 1971; reprint Bonanza, 1990)

Sex and Bacon: Why I Love Things That Are Very, Very Bad for Me, by Sarah Katherine Lewis (Seal Press, 2008)

Adventures of a Bacon Curer, by Maynard (Davies) (Merlin Unwin Books, 2003)

Secrets of a Bacon Curer, by Maynard (Davies) (Merlin Unwin Books, 2007)

In Praise of Irish Breakfasts, by Malachi McCormick (Stone Street Press, 1991)

The Good Fat Cookbook, by Fran McCullough (Scribner, 2007)

Bill Neal's Southern Cooking, by Bill Neal (University of North Carolina Press, 1989)

Bacon and Hams, by George J. Nicholls (The Institute of Certificated Grocers, 1917; reprint 1924)

Everything Tastes Better with Bacon, by Sara Perry (Chronicle Books, 2002)

Seduced by Bacon, by Joanna Pruess (Lyons Press, 2006)

The Hotel Butcher, Garde Manger and Carver, by Frank Rivers et al. (Hotel Monthly Press, 1916)

Charcuterie: The Craft of Salting, Smoking, and Curing, by Michael Ruhlman and Brian Polcyn (W. W. Norton, 2005)

Tree Crops: A Permanent Agriculture, by J. Russell Smith (Harcourt, Brace and Co., 1929; reprint Devin-Adair Company, 1950; reprint Island Press, 1987)

Roadfood Sandwiches, by Jane and Michael Stern (Houghton Mifflin Harcourt, 2007)

"Enhancing Pork Flavor and Fat Quality with Swine Raised in Sylvan Systems: Potential Niche-Market Application for the Ossabaw Hog," by Charles W. Talbott, M. Todd See, Peter Kaminsky, Don Bixby, Michael Sturek, I. Lehr Brisbin and Charles Kadzere, in *Renewable Agriculture and Food Systems* (2006), volume 3, number 21: pages 183–191.

Pigs: From Cave to Corn Belt, by Charles Wayland Towne and Edward Norris Wentworth (University of Oklahoma Press, 1950)

The Bacon Cookbook, by James Villas (Wiley, 2007)

The Foxfire Book, edited by Eliot Wigginton (Anchor Press, 1967)

Appreciations

It's kind of a given that I'm going to forget to thank at least one of the people who've helped get this thing to where it is. So let me just a) apologize up front for forgetting you, and b) say that I feel incredibly fortunate to work in a setting—here at Zingerman's and in the food world at large—filled with so many generous, intelligent, creative and caring people. I really, really appreciate having the opportunity to work with and learn from all of you every day!

In particular I want to appreciate the bacon makers and suppliers: Sam Edwards, Tanya Nueske, Allan Benton, Ronny and Beth Drennan, Mr. Bende, William Johnson, Ken Haviland, Fingal Ferguson, Bruce Aidells, Steven Burger, Herb Eckhouse, everyone at Salumi in Seattle, Paul Bertolli, Sharon Meehan, Meghan Meehan, Bill Robertson, Ron Nodine, Charlie Gatton, Nancy Newsom, Brendan at Tommy Maloney's, Ed Reiser and Melvin Ling.

Then there are all the people who helped me track down information, shared stories, encouraged me and listened to more than they probably wanted to know about bacon: William Tullberg, Randolph Hodgson, Molly Stevens, John T. Edge, Angie Mosier, April McGreger, Francois Vecchio, Fred Sauceman, Paul Willis, Joeli Yaguda, Bob Perry, Tony Spicer, Tricia Gatza, Evan and Julien, Doe Coover, Brooke Keesling, Meg Noori, Phil Deloria, Michael Witgen, Peter Foynes, Amy Evans and last but totally not least, Mary Beth Lasseter.

Of course there are all the writers and musicians who I learned from: Harriette Arnow, George Lang, Maynard Davies, Francine Maroukian, Elizabeth Minchilli, Sarah Katherine Lewis, Uncle Earl and Andre Williams.

Then there are the people who do all the behind-the-scenes work to make this thing a reality: the purchasing crew at the Deli, Gauri Thergaonkar, Rodger Bowser, Julio Vanderpool, Kieron Hales and Bill Wallo. Also the entire Zingerman's Marketing and Graphics Crew: Pete

Sickman-Garner, Nicole Robichaud, Ian Nagy, Ryan Stiner, Billie Lee, Raúl Peña, Betsy Bruner and Courtney Ceronsky for all their great design work.

Special thanks to Jean Henry and Jenny Tubbs for everything from diligent recipe testing to researching the thickness of a fourpence coin. Also to Ann Lofgren for final-round recipe testing.

Thanks to all the partners at Zingerman's for making it possible for me to be doing a book like this in the first place: Paul, Frank, John, Allen, Steve, Maggie, Amy, Stas', Alex, Grace, Toni, Rick, Tom and Mo.

Special thanks to Jan and Dan Longone for their help and encouragement on this and on so many other projects to learn about food and food history over all the years that we've known each other.

Special appreciation to Jillian Downey who's worked so long, hard and patiently on this project right from the beginning. And to Jim Reische for great editing and the bacon fat mayonnaise.

Ari

About the Author

Ari Weinzweig
Zingerman's Co-Founding Partner

Ari moved to Ann Arbor from his hometown of Chicago to attend the University of Michigan. After graduating with a degree in Russian history, he went to work washing dishes in a local restaurant and soon discovered that he loved the food business. Along with his partner Paul Saginaw, Ari started Zingerman's Delicatessen in 1982 with a $20,000 bank loan, a staff of two, a small selection of great-tasting specialty foods and a relatively short sandwich menu. Today, Zingerman's is an Ann Arbor institution—the source of great food and great experiences for over 500,000 visitors every year. Each day the Deli serves up thousands of made-to-order sandwiches with ingredients like corned beef and pastrami, homemade chopped liver and chicken salad. The Deli stocks an array of farmhouse cheeses, smoked fish, salamis, estate-bottled olive oils, vintage vinegars, whole bean coffees, loose leaf teas and much more.

Ari, Paul and the managing partners of the various Zingerman's businesses have built Zingerman's into an organization with a 500-person staff and annual sales approaching $35,000,000 a year. The Zingerman's Community of Businesses currently includes seven businesses in addition to the Deli:

ZINGERMAN'S BAKEHOUSE, opened in 1992, produces a flavorful array of traditional, hearth-baked breads and scrumptious, buttery pastries.

ZINGERMAN'S MAIL ORDER delivers wonderful traditionally made foods to customers across the country and around the globe. Ed Behr, in *The International Wine Cellar*, referred to the catalog as ". . . the most discriminating mail order selection of foods that I am aware of . . ."

ZINGERMAN'S CATERING and ZINGERMAN'S EVENTS take "The Zingerman's Experience" off-site to deliver everything from elegant entrees to bodacious barbecue.

ZINGTRAIN offers consulting in training systems, customer service, specialty foods management and other disciplines.

ZINGERMAN'S CREAMERY is dedicated to bringing fabulous tasting hand-crafted fresh cheeses, gelato and more to dairy lovers everywhere.

ZINGERMAN'S ROADHOUSE opened in September 2003, serving up really good American food for lunch and dinner, along with a full selection of American-made beers and wines, seven days a week.

ZINGERMAN'S COFFEE COMPANY, started in May 2004, focuses on roasting small batches of single-estate beans.

Ari is involved in many educational activities. He has served as a board member and president of the American Cheese Society and as a board member of the Retail Division of the National Association for the Specialty Food Trade. He is a frequent guest speaker in business classes at the University of Michigan and Eastern Michigan University, as well as at various food and business conferences in this country and abroad including the American Institute of Wine and Food, Oldways Preservation and Exchange Trust, the Gathering of Games and the NASFT Fancy Food Show.

In 1988 Zingerman's was instrumental in the founding of Food Gatherers, a perishable food rescue program, and continues to be a major supporter of the organization. Every year Food Gatherers delivers over a million pounds of food to people in need. Ari has also served on the board of The Ark, the longest continuously operating folk music venue in America. In April of 1995, Ari and Paul received the Jewish Federation of Washtenaw County's first Humanitarian Award for their community contributions. Ari was recognized as one of the "Who's Who of Food & Beverage in America" by the 2006 James Beard Foundation. In 2007, Ari and Paul were presented with the Lifetime Achievement Award from *Bon Appetit* magazine for their work in the food industry.

Ari has written over 200 issues of Zingerman's newsletter, "Zingerman's News," and has contributed to such magazines as *Fine Cooking, Specialty Foods, Gourmet Retailer* and *Food and Wine.* He has received praise for his books: *Zingerman's Guide to Good Olive Oil, Zingerman's Guide to Good Vinegar, Zingerman's Guide to Good Parmigiano-Reggiano, Zingerman's Guide to Giving Great Service* and *Zingerman's Guide to Good Eating.*